Setting for the WPA Theatre production of "A Different Moon."

# A DIFFERENT MOON

BY ARA WATSON

DRAMATISTS
PLAY SERVICE
INC.

FOR SAM

A DIFFERENT MOON was given its New York premiere at the WPA Theatre (Kyle Renick, Artistic Director), in New York City, on January 27, 1983. It was directed by Sam Blackwell; the setting was by Jim Steere; lighting was by Craig Evans; the costumes were by Don Newcomb; and the sound was by Michael Kartzmer. The cast, in order of appearance, was as follows:

TYLER BIARS . . . . . . . . . . . . . . *Christopher Cooper*

RUTH BIARS . . . . . . . . . . . . . . . . . . . . *Zina Jasper*

JEAN BIARS . . . . . . . . . . . . . . . . . . . . *Betsy Aidem*

SARAH JOHNSON . . . . . . . . . . . . *Linda Lee Johnson*

A DIFFERENT MOON was first produced by the Actors Theatre of Louisville (Jon Jory, Producing-Director) at the 6th Humana Festival of New American Plays in February, 1982. It was directed by Sam Blackwell; set design was by Paul Owen; the sound was by Mollysue Wedding; costume design by Jess Goldstein; and the lighting design by Jeff Hill. The cast was as follows:

TYLER . . . . . . . . . . . . . . . . . . . . . . . . . *Bruce Kuhn*

RUTH . . . . . . . . . . . . . . . . . . . . . *Gloria Cromwell*

JEAN . . . . . . . . . . . . . . . . . . . . . . . *Judith Yerby*

SARAH . . . . . . . . . . . . . . . . . . . . . *Penelope Allen*

# CAST OF CHARACTERS

Ruth Biars . . . . . . . . . . . . . . . . . . . . . *45 years old*
Tyler Biars . . . . . . . . . . . . . . . . . . . . . *25 years old*
Jean Biars . . . . . . . . . . . . . . . . . . . . . *17 years old*
Sarah Johnson . . . . . . . . . . . . . . . . . . *34 years old*

*Place:* Masefield, Arkansas
*Time:* Summer, 1951

# A DIFFERENT MOON

## ACT I

### Scene i

TIME: *June, 1951—Early evening after supper*

PLACE: *A small town in Arkansas*

SET: *The front of a one storey white house with a wrap-around front porch. There is a yard space in front of the house and on the side. On the porch is a rocker and there is a screen door leading into the front room of the house. There are about two steps leading from the yard to the porch.*

AT RISE: *The stage is empty. In the distance we hear the sound of children playing. Under this sound are other evening sounds—cicadas, an occasional bird, etc. After a long moment, Tyler walks onto the porch from the house, smoking a cigarette. He is in his mid-twenties, handsome, and is dressed in army fatigues. Tyler possesses an easy charm and an ever ready infectious smile. He stands looking out over the audience. There is a slight increase in the volume of the children and Tyler turns and looks with the in-*

*crease in volume. When the sound reaches this new level, he walks to the edge of the porch, hesitates only a moment and, then, smiles and bounds off the porch just as Ruth enters onto the porch from the house. Ruth is mid-forties, pretty. She is dressed in a simple, but nice dress and heels. She is removing the full apron which covers her dress.*

RUTH. (*Seeing Tyler as he hits the ground.*) Tyler? (*He doesn't hear.*) Ty? (*Tyler stops and turns to her almost startled. She smiles and the sound fades back to its lower level.*) Where you going?
TYLER. Oh-h-h . . . (*He turns to the sound which fades a bit more, then quickly back to her. Smiles.*) I don't know.
RUTH. Surely going there in a hurry.
TYLER. You know me, ma. (*Comes back to porch.*) Guess I thought I might . . oh go for a walk, maybe . . . maybe go play a little "kick-the-can" with those kids . . .
RUTH. (*Teasingly.*) In those boots?
TYLER. (*Looks down, laughs.*) You think I might do some damage to the can?
RUTH. It's possible . . but I was thinking more about the damage the can might do to that . . that spit and polish shine you spent the afternoon putting on. (*They smile at each other. Ruth hangs the apron on the back of the rocker and sits.*)
TYLER. (*Looking off.*) The thing is, when I jumped off that porch I was barefoot. Barefoot and ready to run like the wind.
RUTH. Were you? Well, I came along just in time to save you from a big disappointment then.
TYLER. What's that?
RUTH. Oh-h-h . . .
TYLER. Don't think they'd let me play with them?
RUTH. Sure . . but they'd be aware the whole time that you didn't fit in, didn't really belong with them . . and . . and

6

you'd be aware of just how tall you really are. (*They look at each other a brief moment, then both laugh.*)

TYLER. Why, you old philosopher you.

RUTH. Just plain country wisdom. (*Their laughter dies. Tyler stares at the sky and Ruth continues looking at him.*) I'm going to miss your laugh.

TYLER. I'll laugh a lot for you in the next three weeks. How about that?

RUTH. It's just that you'll be gone so long this time . . .

TYLER. (*Moves away.*) I'll be back before you know it.

RUTH. I only wish it weren't . . that you weren't going there. It's so —

TYLER. (*Interrupting.*) Hey. I thought we had an agreement.

RUTH. The name even sounds like war — Korea. War. Can't you write to someone? I'm sure if you —

TYLER. You know I can't. (*Ruth starts to say something, but he stops her.*) Listen . . you remember what I told you would happen if you ever even brought this subject up again, don't you? (*Ruth gives him a look of disdain and a discounting wave of the hand.*) Oh-ho. Have no faith in what your son says? Guess I just have to teach you a lesson — you leave me no choice. (*He slowly raises his hands, extends them toward her and begins wiggling his fingers at her. Slowly he begins advancing on her.*)

RUTH. (*Not to be intimidated.*) Oh, Tyler. Now, I'm serious.

TYLER. (*Closer.*) Me, too. (*He begins making "gitchey-goo", tickling sounds.*)

RUTH. (*Giggles.*) I mean it, now. You're being silly. (*He comes closer and she laughs.*) Tyler. (*Ruth starts to rise, but Tyler leaps at her causing her to curl back into her chair in self protection. Her laughter grows 'til it is quite loud as Tyler's hands play frantically near her body, but never actually touch her.*) Tyler . . . I mean . . it . . Tyler . . don't . . don't you dare . . . (*A laughing scream.*) Ty-y-y-ler!

(*Tyler and Ruth are both laughing — Tyler at the sounds and contortions his mother is making — when Jean appears at the screen door. She is seventeen and very pretty. She is dressed in casual clothes and has a few pin curls in her hair. She is barefoot.*)

JEAN. (*Appearing.*) What on earth?! (*Opens the door, but only steps a half step out.*) Mother! Tyler, stop that! Honestly, you two. . . . Someone will call the fire department out.

TYLER. (*Pulling back from Ruth.*) Well . . how about trying for the Sheriff, too . . . (*And he jumps after Jean.*)

JEAN. (*Running back into the house — reprovingly.*) Tyler!

TYLER. (*Left holding the screen door — laughingly calls after her.*) This is what happens when you keep a man waiting. (*Winks at Ruth, who is recovering in the chair.*) Got to keep my hands busy.

RUTH. (*Wiping the tears.*) You're not funny. (*Tyler wiggles his fingers at her again and she's ready to collapse into laughter.*) Tyler! (*Tyler smiles at her, then walks to the edge of the porch, lights a cigarette as Ruth pulls herself back together.*)

TYLER. (*Listening.*) They've stopped.

RUTH. We probably scared them all to death.

TYLER. They've moved to the creek is all. Catching crawdaddies.

RUTH. What time are you supposed to be at your friend's party?

TYLER. Not my friends, ma. Just kids.

RUTH. Better not let Miz Jeannie hear that. She considers herself quite grown-up this summer. Of course, she thought she was grown-up at three also. Could I have one of those?

TYLER. Sure. (*Gives her a cigarette and lights it for her.*) She sure is a beautiful girl, isn't she?

RUTH. Always was. Both of my children were beautiful from the day they were born. Ty, you know if you don't want to go with Jeannie to this party tonight, you certainly don't have to. You can stay with me and we'll—

TYLER. No, no. I don't mind. Besides, she's been begging me every night since I got home last week.

RUTH. She wants to show you off. She's very proud of you.

TYLER. I think she's trying to fix me up with one of her friends.

RUTH. Well, now, that's something. I didn't know she had any friends she'd think were good enough for her big brother.

TYLER. Who's Vicky?

RUTH. Vicky. Vicky Holbrook.

TYLER. (*Recognition.*) Ah.

RUTH. (*Teasing.*) Not a bad match.

TYLER. She was a good looking kid. Maybe this'll be all right.

RUTH. Her mother is a very good and a very old friend of mine, Tyler Justin Biars, and don't you forget it. (*Tyler smiles at Ruth in humorous understanding of her meaning. Slight pause.*)

TYLER. (*Looking out.*) I think I'll take a short walk while our Jeannie's "preparing" herself.

RUTH. (*Stands.*) Want some company?

TYLER. I'm just going down to the creek . . .

RUTH. That's fine. (*Turns toward door.*) Let me tell—

TYLER. I'll only be gone a minute.

RUTH. (*Realizing.*) Oh.

TYLER. Your shoes might . . .

RUTH. (*Smiles.*) You go ahead.

TYLER. (*Moving away.*) Come if you want to.

RUTH. No. Go on. I'll . . stay and hurry Jean along.

TYLER. Be back . . . (*Exits. Ruth stands watching him go. The evening sounds fade up a bit until Jean appears at the door, then back down under her.*)

JEAN. (*Appearing.*) Mother . . ? Mother, could you—Where's Tyler? (*She steps just outside the screen door.*)

RUTH. He'll be back.

JEAN. Where'd he go?

RUTH. Just off by himself for a few minutes. What do you need, honey?

JEAN. Well, could you come over here? I don't want everyone to see me like this.

RUTH. You look perfectly fine to me.

JEAN. I've still got bobby pins in my hair.

RUTH. (*Moves to her.*) What can I do?

JEAN. My zipper's stuck. (*Ruth drops her cigarette to the porch and puts it out with her foot. She gets the zipper unstuck without much effort.*) Thank you. (*Jean quickly and easily bends down and picks the cigarette butt up and blows the ashes away with one breath.*)

RUTH. (*Smiles down at her and her compulsiveness.*) You about ready?

JEAN. (*Rising, she reaches over and gets the apron.*) I have to iron my blouse and get dressed is all. (*She starts in neatly folding the apron.*)

RUTH. I ironed that white eyelet before supper.

JEAN. Oh? Oh, well, it must have just gotten a little wrinkled . . hanging in the closet. Thank you, anyway. (*Exits into the house.*)

RUTH. (*Smiles after her—looks out to where Tyler exited— to herself.*) Whose little girl are you? (*Exits into the house, calling after Jean.*) What time are you supposed to be there? (*The stage is empty a long moment during which we hear far off in the distance the crescendo of children's playing laughter. As it fades again, Sarah enters carring a small suitcase. Sarah is in her mid-thirties, has a plain but sweet face and a roundish body. She is dressed in a full skirt, sleeveless blouse, flat shoes, and a small hat. Sarah walks slowly past the house, looking at it. She stops and after a moment of staring at the house she takes a deep breath and walks up to the porch. She sets the suitcase down next to it so that it is not seen when one is standing on the porch. She goes up one*) *of the steps, then retreats a few steps into the yard. Ruth enters onto the porch. Sarah turns at the sound. Ruth, pleasantly:*) Hello.

SARAH. Hello.

RUTH. Were you . . looking for someone . . . ?

SARAH. (*Quickly.*) No. I mean . . yes. No. (*She looks down, then out over the audience.*)

RUTH. (*Slight pause.*) Well, it surely is a lovely evening for a walk.

SARAH. Surely is.

RUTH. Didn't get too hot today. 'Course it never gets too hot here because we're in this valley like this . . we've got the mountains so close. (*Looks at her.*) Are you . . visiting . . around here?

SARAH. (*Turning to her.*) My name is Sarah Johnson.

RUTH. No, I don't believe I know any Johnsons. (*Ruth comes off the porch into the yard.*) Dilman Johnson, but they moved about, oh . . before my father died anyway. (*Extends her hand.*) I'm Ruth Biars.

SARAH. (*Shaking.*) How do you do? I'm Sarah Johnson. (*Realizes.*) Oh . .

RUTH. Hello, Sarah. I have an older sister named Sara— Sara Leatrice.

SARAH. I'm Sarah Anne.

RUTH. That's a lovely name.

SARAH. Thank you.

RUTH. Masefield is a very nice place to visit in June. One of our prettiest months. Did . . your people come from here . . or . . . ?

SARAH. No.

RUTH. Just visiting friends, then. I know 'bout everybody—

SARAH. Miz Biars? I was wondering . . is . . is your son at home?

RUTH. My son? You mean Tyler?

SARAH. Yes. Is Tyler here right now?

11

RUTH. Tyler? Well . . no. No, I'm afraid he isn't.

SARAH. Oh.

RUTH. Not this very minute he's. . . Where . . where do you know my Tyler from?

SARAH. Georgia.

RUTH. Georgia?

SARAH. Tyler was in Georgia.

RUTH. Yes, I—

SARAH. Tyler and my little brother are in the army. They went to jump school together in the army in Georgia.

RUTH. Oh-h-h. Your brother's a friend of my son's? Well, what do you know?

SARAH. And Tyler used to come out to our house sometimes . . . to my parent's farm . . I live out there . . and he came out with my brother and . . and he said . . Tyler said that if I ever wanted to . . to come visit here . . he said. . . . Do you know when he'll be back?

RUTH. No . . not exactly, I don't. Did you. . . Is Tyler expecting you today or . . .

SARAH. I wrote you a letter. I mean, Tyler. I wrote Tyler . . .

RUTH. I'm sorry if I seem . . It's just that he didn't say anything to me about—

SARAH. (*Opening purse.*) No. No, see, I didn't . . . (*Takes letter out.*) I forgot to mail it.

RUTH. Oh. Yes.

SARAH. I . . I found it in my purse on the bus . . .

RUTH. Well . . you must be awfully tired if you just got off a bus ride all the way from Georgia. I know—

SARAH. I've been on it for four days.

RUTH. On the bus?

SARAH. Yes.

RUTH. From Georgia? That seems—

SARAH. No, but I . . I bought the wrong ticket at that bus station is how come.

RUTH. (*Sympathetically.*) Oh, no.

SARAH. I went to Louisiana first . . to Masefield, Louisiana,

12

instead of Masefield here . . So that's why it took me four days.

RUTH. You . . have to be careful about . . that sort of . . . There must be quite a few towns named Masefield . . (*Sarah nods, looking down at the ground. Ruth stares at her with a slight sense of bewilderment.*)

JEAN. (*Appearing at the door.*) Mother?

RUTH. (*Turns, startled.*) Jeannie?

JEAN. (*Steps onto the porch.*) I didn't mean to scare you.

RUTH. No . .

JEAN. (*To Sarah.*) Hello.

SARAH. Hello.

RUTH. Sarah . . this . . this is my daughter Jean. Jeannie, this is Sarah Johnson.

SARAH. Hello.

RUTH. Sarah is . . Sarah's brother and Tyler were in jump school together. (*Smiles at Sarah.*) In Georgia.

SARAH. Yes. They're real good friends. Ben . . that's my brother's . . .

JEAN. (*Has never heard this name before.*) Ben?

RUTH. Ben.

JEAN. Ben. Yes.

RUTH. And . . Sarah here has . . has come for a little visit with us.

JEAN. A visit? Oh . . . well . . that's . . real nice. Isn't it, mother?

RUTH. Yes. Won't that be nice?

SARAH. Tyler told me he had a sister.

JEAN. I guess that's me.

SARAH. He said you were "pretty as a picture." You are.

JEAN. Thank you. That's . . .

SARAH. (*To Ruth.*) Do you have any more kids?

RUTH. Just the two. (*Sees the suitcase.*) Is this yours?

SARAH. Yes.

RUTH. Now, that was a quite silly question, wasn't it?

SARAH. No. (*Ruth picks up the bag. It is very light.*) I can—
RUTH. I've already got it. And you're just going to have to forgive my rudeness, Sarah, for making you stand out here. I don't know where my mind was. (*Moves toward door.*) You just follow me right on inside. Maybe you'd like to take a cool bath . . change your clothes . . .
SARAH. Yes, I would. I feel real dirty.
RUTH. (*Holding door open.*) You come with me and I'll show you your room and fix you a bite to eat while—just step right on in—(*Sarah steps into the house.*) Jean? (*Ruth continues to hold door, but moves toward Jean as far as she can.*) Honey, maybe you wouldn't mind walking down around the bridge and seeing if your brother's anywhere near there. Tell him we've got company.
SARAH. (*Leaning out.*) Don't tell him who is it, though.
RUTH. I think maybe we better. Don't you, Sarah? Might get him up here quicker. (*Sarah looks at Ruth and, then, moves on into the house. To Jean:*) Run on.
JEAN. What about the party?
RUTH. We can talk about that later. (*Jean stares at her.*) It'll be all right. Don't worry about it. (*Jean turns and walks quickly, exiting D.L. Ruth turns in toward the house.*) Give you some time to freshen up. (*Entering the house.*) Your room will be through the hall there. (*Her voice fades.*) I've got some meatloaf I can warm up for you. You haven't had supper. . . . (*The voice fades and we are left with the evening sounds at their normal level for a long moment. Then the sounds begin to fade up as the lights fade down.*)

# ACT I

## Scene ii

*TIME: Late night of the same day*

*SET: The same*

*AT RISE: The lights and sound are held for a long
moment at the end of the previous scene, then the
lights come up on a clear white night and the sounds
become muted night sounds. There is a dim light
coming from a lamp in the house. After a long moment, Tyler appears dressed as he was at the top of
the act. He moves toward the house and stops at the
corner of the porch, stands and listens and, then,
gives three short whistles. After a moment, he gives
them again. Ruth appears at the door, steps onto the
porch, closing the screen quietly behind her. She
looks around and sees Tyler. They look at each other
a brief moment and, then, she walks off the porch
and to him quickly and quietly.*

RUTH. (*After a brief pause.*) Where on earth have you
been? I have been worried sick.
TYLER. Walking.
RUTH. Walking? For the last four hours? I've called all over
this town.

TYLER. I went out to the graveyard.

RUTH. To the graveyard?

TYLER. Did she leave yet?

RUTH. And just how did you even know she was here?

TYLER. Jeannie told me.

RUTH. Jean told me she couldn't find you.

TYLER. I asked her to say that.

RUTH. (*Takes him by the arm and moves him farther from the porch.*) I don't like this, Tyler. I do not like this one bit.

TYLER. Ma, you knew I'd be o.k.

RUTH. I do not like you asking your sister to lie for you and I do not—

TYLER. I'm sorry, ma. I really am. I shouldn't've done it, but . . but I needed . . Is she still here?

RUTH. Sarah? Of course, she's still here. Did you think she'd just go away, disappear? (*Brief pause.*) You've put me in a most awkward and uncomfortable position, Tyler.

TYLER. I didn't mean to do that, mother. You know I didn't. Is Jean back yet?

RUTH. No.

TYLER. I told her I'd meet her at the party.

RUTH. Oh, Tyler.

TYLER. Maybe I better—

RUTH. Jean will be all right. We have some talking to do right here, you and I.

TYLER. Yeah. (*Brief pause.*) Where is she? Sarah?

RUTH. She's asleep. The poor thing sat up in there waiting for you 'til. . . Do you want to tell me what this is all about?

TYLER. Nothing. It's not about anything.

RUTH. It has to be about something.

TYLER. She's crazy. I don't mean she's crazy. She's just. . . Really, ma . . I can't believe she's done this. . . The story is . . the story is I went out to her folks' house with Ben . . Ben's her brother . . about three, four times, maybe . . and she was there . . because she lives there I guess . . and

16

. . and, you know, I was nice to her because . . . her family was nice to me and I took her out a couple of times, I guess — and one of those times was even with Ben — and she got this . . crush on me. So I quit going out there. I hardly even know her.

RUTH. She said you invited her here.

TYLER. I didn't. I wouldn't. Oh, maybe I said one of those things you say, but. . . Ma, look, it got to the point that I had to tell her — she started writing me these letters every day and, then, she started calling me and all the guys in my company started kidding me about it . . and it just got to the point that I had to tell people, tell the guys, to tell her I wasn't there when she called.

RUTH. Did you ask her to stop?

TYLER. It wouldn't have done any good. She's . . I don't know what she is. I'm just real sorry you had to get involved in it. but I never thought in a million years she'd do something like this. You know . . she comes from . . dirt farmers . . they're good people, but I think she thought I . . looked pretty good . . or something . . (*Smiles at Ruth.*) That's the problem with having good-lookin' kids, ma . . see . . people chase after 'em.

RUTH. She chased you a long way.

TYLER. Whew. (*Goes to Ruth and puts an arm around her.*) I tell you what I'll do. In the morning I'll have a good long talk with her and, then, I'll get her on the first bus out of here — I mean I won't be rude or anything, but . . I promise you won't have to —

RUTH. Tyler, when you left Georgia, did you know she was going to have a baby? (*Tyler looks at her a long moment, then walks a few feet away.*)

TYLER. Did she tell you that?

RUTH. No.

TYLER. How do you know she's telling the truth?

RUTH. I said she didn't.

TYLER. (*Turns to her.*) You just guessing?

17

RUTH. No. Partly.

TYLER. Does she look . . ?

RUTH. Not very.

TYLER. Maybe she isn't, then.

RUTH. Tyler.

TYLER. Could Jean tell?

RUTH. I don't think so.

TYLER. Jesus. Jesus, Jesus.

RUTH. It . . it is . . yours, then?

TYLER. I don't know. She said . . I don't know.

RUTH. Tyler, Tyler, Tyler. How could you do this to yourself?

TYLER. (*Shrugs.*) Wasn't intentional.

RUTH. These things seldom are. That doesn't mean—

TYLER. Please don't mother. I feel real bad. Real bad.

RUTH. Oh, Tyler . . I know you do. I don't mean to make it worse for you than . . While I was waiting for you tonight, I thought about telling her that I'd gotten a message from you . . . that you'd left, you weren't ever coming back, so she might just as well . . .

TYLER. That was almost the truth. I almost did that. I almost hitched right on out of here tonight. I wanted to.

RUTH. It wouldn't have solved anything.

TYLER. I sat out in the graveyard and I—

RUTH. That is so morbid, sitting in a graveyard at night, Tyler. That is just so morbid.

TYLER. Naw. I like it out there. My favorite hiding place when I was a kid.

RUTH. This isn't something you can hide from.

TYLER. I wasn't. I only needed someplace quiet to . . sort things out.

RUTH. And have you?

TYLER. Sure. Mostly.

RUTH. (*Takes a deep breath.*) What are you going to do?

TYLER. I haven't . . But I know I have to take care of it and I will and I promise you I'll do what's best. I just wish you wouldn't be so mad at me.

RUTH. I'm not.

TYLER. You look a little mad.

RUTH. Well, I have every right to be. You could have had any girl in the—

TYLER. (*Goes to her.*) Ma. Come on. Please. I hate to see you like this. It'll be all right. Hey, girlfriend, you don't want to waste a beautiful night like this, do you? I know what we can do. Let's pull out that bottle of bourbon and let's get drunk and sing— (*Sarah appears at the screen door. She is barefoot, her clothes wrinkled.*)

SARAH. Tyler? Tyler, is that— (*Enters onto porch. Ruth instinctively steps between them in protectiveness of Tyler and is immediately aware of having done so.*)

RUTH. Sarah.

TYLER. Hello, Sarah.

SARAH. (*Shyly.*) Hello, Tyler. I fell asleep.

RUTH. You were exhausted. She was just exhausted, Tyler.

SARAH. Where did you go?

TYLER. Me? I . . I ran into an old buddy. (*Moves toward her.*) Well, welcome to Masefield. This is quite a surprise. (*He gives her a quick kiss on the cheek.*) Would you look at you?

SARAH. I look bad?

TYLER. No, I meant . . So. How'd you get here?

SARAH. By bus.

TYLER. I came up by bus. Long ride.

SARAH. Yes, it is. (*Slight pause.*)

RUTH. Were you cool enough in your room, Sarah? Tonight?

SARAH. Yes. I'm glad to see you, Tyler.

TYLER. Me, too. Me, too. I . . wish you'd written me, though. If I'd a' known you was comin', I'd a' baked a cake.

SARAH. I did. I did write, didn't I, Miz Biars? Want to see it? I'll go—

RUTH. Never you mind, Sarah. (*Attempting to cover the*

*awkwardness.*) Besides, I've tasted Tyler's cooking.

TYLER. Oh-ho.

SARAH. But I could go—

RUTH. And when it comes to letter writing—

TYLER. Hey, give me a break . .

SARAH. Tyler doesn't like to write letters, do you?

RUTH. (*Slight awkward pause.*) Well . . no . . he's not very . . but . . but I made him promise. When he went away this last time, I made him promise he'd write me at least once a week. And he did. Except he never mailed any of them.

SARAH. Did you really write them?

RUTH. Oh, yes, he really did. When he got home the bottom of his suitcase was filled with them—in the envelopes, sealed, addressed . . no stamps, though.

TYLER. Stamps are very expensive things these days.

RUTH. I would have sent you the money.

TYLER. I never found out where the post office was.

SARAH. (*Sincerely—not understanding the banter.*) Ben could have showed you. There was one right on the post. (*Ruth and Tyler exchange an uncomfortable look.*)

RUTH. He's only trying to find some excuse, but he can't. (*Smiles at Tyler.*) I'm enjoying reading them now, though. Like reading a diary.

SARAH. Did you read about me?

RUTH. I . . haven't finished reading them, yet . . .

SARAH. You ought to save them all when you get done.

RUTH. I will.

SARAH. I know a girl in our town who was engaged to a boy who worked for a . . you know, he built roads and he drove one of those big . . big yellow machines—

TYLER. Road-grader?

SARAH. Something like that. And he wrote letters to her all the time and she saved them in a little box that she kept locked and one day that machine rolled over with him on it and he got killed and when she opened that box, after the funeral, there was nothing but ashes in it. That's all. (*Slight pause.*)

RUTH. You . . do hear . . about things like that . . sometimes . . .

TYLER. How's your folks?

SARAH. They're fine.

TYLER. How's your brother? How's Ben?

SARAH. Fine.

TYLER. Good. I'm glad to hear that.

SARAH. Ben's off on a fishing trip right now.

TYLER. Sounds great.

SARAH. (*Smiles.*) Ben loves to fish. He doesn't know I'm here right now.

TYLER. Oh?

SARAH. No, he doesn't even know.

TYLER. You tell him hello for me when he gets back. (*Slight pause.*)

RUTH. Well, if . . if you two will excuse me I think I'd better— (*Jean enters. She is prettily dressed. Ruth, seeing Jean, to Tyler:*) Your sister.

TYLER. (*Turning.*) Hey, here she is. (*He quickly moves down to where she has stopped.*) Wow. You look like a million. (*Close to her, he lowers his voice.*) I'm sorry, kid.

JEAN. You said you'd come later.

TYLER. Please? I was looking forward to it, too.

JEAN. I waited.

TYLER. I'll make it up to you.

RUTH. (*From porch.*) How was your party, honey?

JEAN. (*Head high, she moves past Tyler toward porch.*) It was wonderful. The best party I've ever been to. (*To Sarah.*) Hello.

SARAH. (*Shyly.*) Hello.

RUTH. Did you walk home all by yourself?

JEAN. Mother, don't make it sound like I crossed the Andes by myself. Peyton walked me part way.

TYLER. (*Following her.*) Ah-ha . . . Peyton.

JEAN. He's not my boyfriend, Tyler.

TYLER. No?

JEAN. No.

RUTH. Don't tease her about boys, Tyler. She doesn't like it.

SARAH. I bet she has lots of boyfriends.

JEAN. I do not.

SARAH. I mean, I . . I bet all the boys around here want to be your boyfriend.

JEAN. I don't care if they do.

RUTH. (*Warningly.*) Jean.

JEAN. Well, I don't.

TYLER. And why not?

JEAN. Because they *are* from around here and they're going to stay from around here.

TYLER. You going someplace?

JEAN. (*Defiantly.*) Yes.

TYLER. Where?

JEAN. (*Angry, on the verge of tears.*) You're not the only one who wants to go off and go places, Tyler.

RUTH. Honey—

JEAN. Well, he's not . . . (*The tears begin and she starts to run toward the door.*)

TYLER. (*Catches her.*) Hey, Jeannie . . Hey, I'm sorry. Really.

JEAN. No, you're not. You always say you are, but—

TYLER. I do mean it. I do.

RUTH. Honey, Ty just wants to make up with you.

JEAN. He shouldn't tease me then.

RUTH. And he wanted to come over to your party, but I wanted to talk to him.

TYLER. (*Putting his arm around Jean, he walks her D.*) See? Wasn't all my fault, kid. (*Ruth looks at Sarah asking understanding with her smile.*)

SARAH. My brother and I fight a lot.

TYLER. Not me and Jeannie. Huh, kid? We never fought,

did we? We were always best friends, weren't we? (*Jean nods.*) I didn't mean to hurt your feelings. I wouldn't do that for the world. Might— (*He pokes her in the ribs gently.*) — rib you a little.

JEAN. (*A giggle.*) Don't.

TYLER. Look, I'm on your side about the guys around here. You're too good for 'em.

JEAN. I'm not either.

TYLER. Hey . . . if you really want to go someplace, I know how you can do it. Join the army.

JEAN. (*Slight defiance.*) I might.

RUTH. No, you won't.

TYLER. Sure, ma. Then maybe we could get an assignment together—become a famous KP team.

JEAN. (*Giggles.*) Silly. Ladies don't join the army.

TYLER. What do ladies do, then?

RUTH. They get to bed at a decent hour, that's what they do, so they can get up and go to church the next day.

JEAN. I'm not tired.

TYLER. That's what comes of not having a boyfriend and having to sit in the corner all evening. (*Jean puts her hands on her hips.*) Sorry. Forget that.

JEAN. For your information, Mr. Smart Alec, I did not sit in the corner. I danced all evening long. Every dance . . . almost. So there.

TYLER. Save the last jitterbug for me?

JEAN. As I remember, you weren't there.

TYLER. (*Holds out arms.*) I'm here now.

JEAN. (*Giggles.*) No, silly.

TYLER. Afraid you can't keep up with me? (*Jean hesitates a moment. Tyler looks at her challengingly and begins humming a popular swing tune. She smiles and goes to him and they dance. They dance well together. Tyler does a few "trick" moves causing Jean and Ruth to laugh. Finally, Tyler dances Jean to the porch, swings her up onto it and, then,*)

*he collapses. Ruth and Sarah applaud.*)
JEAN. (*Bending over him.*) Who can't keep up with whom?
TYLER. (*Trying to grab one of her legs.*) Youm.
JEAN. (*Avoiding him.*) Getting old?
TYLER. (*Laughing.*) Yes.
JEAN. Even mother can do better than that.
RUTH. "Even mother"?
JEAN. I didn't—
RUTH. Well, you know, it's hard to dance with one foot in the grave.
JEAN. Oh, mother.
RUTH. Come on. Time for you to hit the hay.
JEAN. (*Going quickly to Tyler.*) Will you go to church with me in the morning?
TYLER. Jean . . .
JEAN. Please?
TYLER. I fall asleep in church.
JEAN. You didn't go to the party with me . . .
TYLER. O.k. O.k., o.k.
JEAN. Will you come to Y.A. class with me?
TYLER. No. Absolutely no. No Sunday School.
JEAN. But I have to go.
TYLER. I'll meet you there. (*Jean looks skeptical.*) I will.
JEAN. (*Smiling.*) All right. Vicky—Vicky?—Vicky'll sit with us.
TYLER. Good.
JEAN. (*Kisses him on the cheek.*) Goodnight. 'Night, mother.
RUTH. I'm right behind you.
JEAN. (*Turns at door—to Sarah.*) Goodnight.
SARAH. (*Happy to be included.*) Goodnight. (*Jean exits. Calling after her.*) Sleep tight. She's . . she's real nice.
RUTH. (*To Tyler.*) What time shall I wake you?
TYLER. *Barely* in time. I'll wake up.
RUTH. Well, I better . . .
TYLER. You don't have to.

RUTH. Yes, I do. I'll see you in the morning. (*Exiting.*) 'Night.

SARAH. Goodnight.

TYLER. 'Night, ma. (*They watch her go. Tyler turns and walks D. and lights a cigarette. Sarah slowly follows.*)

SARAH. It's a beautiful night.

TYLER. Sure is.

SARAH. Not too hot like at home. At home it's . . it's . . hot. I didn't know what else to do, Tyler. I was scared. (*Tyler moves another step or two away — listening.*) I don't want you to be mad —

TYLER. Sh-h-h. (*Gestures at her as he listens and looks out over the audience. Silence for a moment, then, in the distance, the sound of a train whistle.*)

SARAH. Train.

TYLER. Sh-h-h.

SARAH. I rode on a train at night once. (*Tyler moves a step farther away from her. We hear two long calls, getting closer.*)

TYLER. (*Looking out.*) God, what a sound. Makes you want to just go. Not even care where. Just go. (*Realizes what he's said and glances at her. Sarah looks back at him. Tyler looks back out. Slight pause.*)

SARAH. (*Looking out.*) Look. There. You can see the smoke. Like little parachutes. Only going up instead of coming down. (*One long whistle.*) I didn't know what else to do after you ran off like that.

TYLER. I didn't "run off." I came home on furlough.

SARAH. But I didn't know when you were going.

TYLER. You should've. Same as your brother's.

SARAH. But I thought you'd come see me or . . . (*Two long whistles at their peak sound about a half mile away.*)

TYLER. My family was expecting me home.

SARAH. But I thought after we talked — after I told you —

TYLER. Sarah. (*Slight pause.*) You only said you might be.

SARAH. No. I told you I was sure.

25

TYLER. You hadn't even been to a doctor. How could you be sure?

SARAH. Well, I am. I've been to a doctor now and I am. (*Three long receding whistles. They both look after the train.*)

TYLER. You shouldn't have come here without letting me know first. You shouldn't've done that. You've got my mother all upset . . .

SARAH. I didn't tell her anything.

TYLER. Your being here, your presence told her, Sarah. You can't stay here.

SARAH. Where am I going to go?

TYLER. Home.

SARAH. I can't . . (*Begins to cry.*) I can't go home. I . . don't have . . any money . . (*And she covers her face with her hands.*)

TYLER. Don't cry. Crying isn't going to . . . (*Slightly irritated.*) Just don't.

SARAH. (*Wiping her face, but the tears still come for a moment longer.*) I don't mean to. I don't want to. I've cried so much these last few weeks . . I mostly feel dry inside. Then it just starts . . and I can't stop it.

TYLER. Your folks, they know?

SARAH. But they're not mad at you. They're mostly just mad at me.

TYLER. Jeez . . . I thought you said you'd been married before.

SARAH. I was.

TYLER. Well . . you should've known not to let something like this happen.

SARAH. I was only sixteen and it only lasted a few days 'til my daddy found me and—

TYLER. Well, you're not sixteen, now. You're thirty— (*Can't remember.*) —thirty some-odd . .

SARAH. Thirty-four.

26

TYLER. Thirty-four? That's even too old to have a . . .
That's too old.
SARAH. My mother had me when she was thirty-six.
TYLER. And look at her now.
SARAH. There's nothing wrong with my mother.
TYLER. That isn't even the point, Sarah. That's not the
point.
SARAH. What is?
TYLER. The point is that you . . *you* . . *(At a loss for a
brief moment—then.)* It . . it might be . . dangerous for
you. *(Sarah looks at him.)* It might be.
SARAH. It's too late now.
TYLER. Maybe it isn't.
SARAH. *(Realizing.)* Oh, no, Tyler. No. I could never . .
Not ever. Never.
TYLER. All right. All right. *(Tyler turns from her and goes
back to the porch and sits. After a short moment, he sings.)*
　　"If I had the wings of an angel,
　　Over these prison walls I would fly.
　　Right in to the arms of my loved one
　　And there would I willingly die." *
*(Tyler stops singing and lights a cigarette.)*
SARAH. *(Moving slowly, shyly toward him.)* I . . I didn't
know you could sing. You've got a real nice voice.
TYLER. Yeah.
SARAH. I mean it. You really do.
TYLER. I mean it, too. I really know I do.
SARAH. *(Smiles.)* Oh, you do?
TYLER. *(Smiles also.)* Yeah, I do. *(Sarah sits on the porch —
some distance from him.)*
SARAH. Maybe that's what you should be.
TYLER. A singer?
SARAH. Yes.

* Music for song appears at back of playbook.

TYLER. I am a singer. Didn't you hear me just now?

SARAH. No-o-o, a real one.

TYLER. Didn't that sound real?

SARAH. You know what I mean.

TYLER. Well . . maybe I will be. Maybe I'll go to Hollywood and be a big singing movie star. (*He sings a few words of "I Dream of Jeannie."*)

SARAH. She doesn't like me being here, does she?

TYLER. I don't know.

SARAH. Who's Vicky?

TYLER. Vicky?

SARAH. Jean said Vicky'd sit with you in church tomorrow.

TYLER. Friend of hers.

SARAH. Not of yours?

TYLER. (*Defiant.*) Yeah. Mine, too.

SARAH. (*Looking down.*) Oh.

TYLER. (*Relents.*) No. Not of mine.

SARAH. (*Smiles.*) I like your mother.

TYLER. She's a real special lady.

SARAH. Did you grow up here in this house?

TYLER. No.

SARAH. I thought you did. Where did you?

TYLER. In a house on the other side of town mostly. Then we traveled around. Lived in Chicago. All over.

SARAH. Why? (*Tyler answers with a shrug.*) Why'd you come back here?

TYLER. My dad died.

SARAH. We lived out on that farm since I was ten. The only other place I lived since then was when I got married that time but I never got too far away. . . . This is the fartherest I've ever been. You like moving around?

TYLER. Yeah.

SARAH. Me, too. I mean, I think I'd like doing that, too.

TYLER. (*Stands.*) My uncle owns this house. He lets them live here for free. Don't tell her I told you that. Pride. She likes living here . . in this house . . in this town. . . It's where she grew up—her whole family, her mother, her father, her whole history is here. It's her home. She never liked moving around I don't think. Women just don't.

SARAH. Are you going to stay in the army?

TYLER. Probably. I probably will. I don't know.

SARAH. I think the army's a good career opportunity.

TYLER. Whatever happened to . . to that guy you used to see? The one your mother was always talking about?

SARAH. She was just trying to—

TYLER. What was his name?

SARAH. George.

TYLER. George.

SARAH. I quit seeing him after I met you.

TYLER. You should'nt've done that. I told you not to. I think—

SARAH. Tyler, I know what I didn't tell you. Daddy's birddog—Rosie?—had her pups.

TYLER. (*Disinterested.*) Good.

SARAH. You could have one.

TYLER. Sarah, what am I going to do with a birddog in Korea?

SARAH. (*Gets up and moves coquettishly, awkwardly toward him.*) Maybe . . if they'd let you take it . . maybe it could . . keep you warm at night. I go out . . to where they are in the barn sometimes and . . and let them crawl over my legs. . . They're real warm and their bodies are real soft . . .

TYLER. Don't do that.

SARAH. What? I'm . . not doing anything.

TYLER. Stop acting like that.

SARAH. I was only . . I only want to talk to you, Tyler. That's all. It's hard to talk when . . (*She looks over her shoulder at the door.*) Maybe . . (*Looks at him.*) Maybe we could . . go for a walk. . . Would you like to?

TYLER. Sarah . .

SARAH. (*Moves slightly closer.*) I . . wouldn't mind. I'd like to.

TYLER. No.

SARAH. It can't hurt anything now. It can't.

TYLER. No.

SARAH. I miss you, Tyler. (*Sarah is standing very close to him. They look at each other a long moment, then he roughly takes her in his arms and roughly kisses her two or three times. Finally, he pushes her away from him. She stands there a brief bewildered moment, then takes him by the hand and starts to try to pull him U.L. He lets her hold his hand a brief moment, then pulls forcefully away and walks D. leaving her crushed. She turns U.*)

TYLER. (*Angry.*) How do I even know it's mine? How do I know it isn't this George's?

SARAH. (*Turning.*) You know. You know.

TYLER. No, I don't. (*Accusingly.*) I'd only met you once. Once. And you'd been seeing that guy for . . for years.

SARAH. I . . never . . (*Starts to cry.*)

TYLER. Stop it. Stop it right now.

SARAH. It's you. It's yours. I swear.

TYLER. You're trying to hang it on me because you think I'm your way out. Well, I'm not.

SARAH. I'm not trying to . . I like you, Tyler. That's why. Nobody else has ever touched me. . . . (*Quiet little voice.*) It *is* yours. It is . . (*Her legs simply will no longer hold her up and she sinks to her knees.*) Oh, my lord . . . My lord, what am I going to do? Somebody . . oh, please . . please, oh, please help me. . . Help me. . . (*Tyler has watched this and only now relents and goes to her.*)

TYLER. Hey . . Sarah . . Come on, now . . (*He tries to help her up.*) Sarah. (*Her legs are unsteady and he picks her up and carries her to the porch where he sets her down. She immediately pulls her knees into her body, encircling them with her arms. She buries her head in her arms. Tyler watches her, lights a cigarette and sits down beside her.*) Hello? Hey, in there. How can I talk to you if I can't see you? (*He puts his hand on her arm.*)

SARAH. (*Lifting her head slightly.*) How can you say that to me?

TYLER. (*Gently teasing.*) 'Cause you've got your head buried.

SARAH. About it's not being yours? How could you? (*Buries her head again.*)

TYLER. (*After a brief pause.*) I shouldn't have . . I was out of line. O.k.? I'm sorry. (*He lifts her chin up.*) I am.

SARAH. My daddy called me a . . . a—

TYLER. He had no business calling you anything. I know you're not. You're a very nice, very sweet girl.

SARAH. Am I?

TYLER. Yes.

SARAH. What are we going to do, Tyler?

TYLER. (*A deep sigh — he moves away.*) What do you want to do?

SARAH. I don't know. I guess . . you know . . .

TYLER. I'm leaving here in two weeks. I'll be gone a year . . almost a year. I couldn't be any help to you . . .

SARAH. Lots of husbands go off.

TYLER. You don't want to marry someone like me. I'm not anywhere near being ready to settle down. Not near. I'm too young for you. I'm not—

SARAH. I'm thinking about the baby.

TYLER. (*Sitting next to her.*) I'm thinking about that, too. What kind of a father would I make? Just think about that—

SARAH. You'd be better than no father. I . . I know you don't love me. I know you don't, even though you said it that time.

TYLER. Oh, Sarah . . (*Up and away.*) . . don't make it sound like I said it just to . . I do . . love you . . but not . . not the kind of love you get married on.

SARAH. You could go wherever you wanted to. I wouldn't

31

mind if we moved around. I'd take real good care of you. People don't have to love each other to be married, Tyler. If we loved our little baby . . .

TYLER. I don't know . . . God . . . A baby . . . (*Stares hard at her.*) It is mine?

SARAH. Yes.

TYLER. Mine.

SARAH. I had a dream about it. It was all wrapped up in a blue blanket.

TYLER. (*Smiles.*) Yeah? (*With some pride.*) I always wanted a . . . (*Stops himself.*) You know, you grow up and you want to have kids . . . I don't know. I don't know what to say or how I feel. I don't know how I feel, Sarah. My mind just keeps skipping around. It doesn't seem to want to stop on any one thing long enough to make any sense of it. Time. I just need some time. We'll work it out.

SARAH. We will?

TYLER. Yes. We'll work it out.

SARAH. (*Looks at him a moment.*) Do you think you could . . .

TYLER. What?

SARAH. Nothing.

TYLER. Tell me.

SARAH. (*Shyly.*) Could you maybe put your arms around me and . . and say that to me? You don't have to . . do anything else. Could you?

TYLER. (*Gently pulling her to him.*) We'll work it all out, Sarah. (*Holds her a moment longer, then pushes her gently back and smiles at her.*) So wipe that worried look off your face.

SARAH. (*Smiles.*) When?

TYLER. I thought that's all you wanted me to say. Look, you've had all this time to think this through and I need to do that, too. And we need to talk some more—

SARAH. I could talk all night.

TYLER. Not to me you couldn't. I'm beat. Besides, aren't

you supposed to be getting a lot of rest and stuff? You are, aren't you? (*Sarah smiles and nods.*) Well, let's get to it, then.

SARAH. But I want—

TYLER. Nope. Tomorrow. Tomorrow we'll get up and have a nice big breakfast and—

SARAH. I can only eat crackers in the morning.

TYLER. Well, maybe in the afternoon we'll go on a picnic. You can eat in the afternoon o.k.?

SARAH. (*Nods.*) All of us?

TYLER. Whatever. (*Sarah smiles lovingly at him.*) Just don't . . push anything, Sarah. It'll be all right. I promise. Now, go on. (*Sarah walks to the door, opens it and turns.*)

SARAH. I don't feel scared now, Tyler.

TYLER. Good.

SARAH. Goodnight.

TYLER. See you tomorrow. (*Sarah exits. Tyler watches her go, then reaches in his pocket and pulls out his cigarettes. He finds the package empty and wads it up as he walks slowly D. He plays with the wadded-up pack by batting it around almost unconsciously. He stops, looks up at the moon and the sky as the lights fade down and night sounds increase. The lights go out.*)

# ACT II

## Scene i

*TIME: The next morning — Sunday*

*SET: The front room of the Biars' home. There is a screen door to the kitchen and an exit U. into the hallway leading to the bedrooms. There are two windows. The room is furnished with a sofa, two chairs, two end tables, a radio and a lamp. On the set at rise is a small Bible, a family photo and a telephone. The set should give the impression of a faded memory in which only the bare essentials stand out.*

*AT RISE: It is a bright summer morning. There are the morning sounds of birds. Sarah is entering from the hallway. She is dressed in a similar outfit to the day before only the wrinkles in this one were caused by being in the suitcase. She walks to the middle of the room and stands a moment looking around at the furniture and objects. She walks to one of the tables on which is a family picture. Just as she reaches to pick it up, Jean enters from the hall. Sarah turns as though she has been caught stealing and both women look at each other for a short moment with the summer sounds raised in volume for that moment. The sound lowers and Jean smiles her grownup, hostess smile. Jean is dressed for church.*

34

JEAN. Good morning.

SARAH. Good morning. I was . . . Is this a picture of your family?

JEAN. My mother's family.

SARAH. Oh.

JEAN. I hope you slept well.

SARAH. Oh, yes, I did. I did sleep very well. Did you?

JEAN. Yes, thank you. (*She crosses in front of Sarah and goes to a table where she picks up a bible.*)

SARAH. You on your way to church?

JEAN. Yes. (*Jean almost unconsciously straightens or rearranges objects in the room during this exchange.*) So . . I'll see you when I get back . . unless you . . (*Stops and looks at Sarah.*) . . were planning on . . or had to leave this morning or . . .

SARAH. No . . I'll probably . . be here . . when you get . . home . .

JEAN. Good. (*Straightening again.*) I was just afraid you might get off without my saying how nice it was to meet you . . .

SARAH. It was nice to meet you, too . . .

RUTH. (*Entering from kitchen.*) Sarah. I didn't expect to see you up for awhile.

SARAH. I didn't mean to sleep so late.

RUTH. Not late at all. Are you hungry? (*Sarah shakes her head.*) Maybe just a piece of toast?

SARAH. Maybe.

RUTH. (*Holding the kitchen door open for Sarah.*) You come on in here with me and I'll see if I can't talk you into—

JEAN. Mother? (*Ruth turns.*) I have to go. Is my slip showing?

RUTH. No. (*To Sarah who is now standing in the doorway.*) You go ahead and take a seat at the table, Sarah. (*Sarah exits. To Jean.*) It's early, isn't it?

JEAN. I have to go over my lesson.

RUTH. Have your offering?

JEAN. (*Quietly.*) Is she staying? (*Ruth nods and indicates Jean is to drop the subject. More quietly.*) For how long?

RUTH. (*Moving to her.*) Your bow isn't quite straight. Let me — (*Quietly.*) Behave yourself. (*Jean gives a heavy sigh. Ruth touches the bow.*) There. Perfect.

JEAN. (*Facing her mother.*) You won't let him forget? Or back out? He promised.

RUTH. I will see that he's there. I'll wake him as soon —

JEAN. He's already up. I do look all right?

RUTH. Very pretty.

JEAN. And make sure he wears his uniform.

RUTH. Uniform.

JEAN. And I'll meet him on the front steps before church service.

RUTH. The front steps.

JEAN. (*Taking Ruth by the arm and moving her to the screen door.*) Don't let her come with him, mother.

RUTH. Jean —

JEAN. Please?

RUTH. No. I'm not going to stop someone from going to church. (*Jean starts to say something, but Ruth holds a warning hand up.*)

JEAN. (*Sighs.*) All right. (*More quietly.*) But I hope she doesn't. (*She opens the door.*) Tell him ten-thirty. I'll help you with dinner when I get home and let *me* set the table. Bye. (*Exits.*)

RUTH. Toodle-do. (*She smiles after her, then turns toward the kitchen and the smile fades. She exits into the kitchen to the slightly raised morning sounds. Just as she exits into the kitchen the sound of a mockingbird begins and runs his repertoire during the next scene. Tyler enters from the hall in dress uniform and stands just inside the doorway until the swinging kitchen door stops swinging. He then steps into the room a few steps looking toward the kitchen and stands only a brief moment. He goes back to the hall entrance, pulling*)

36

*his cloth cap from his back pocket and putting it on. He
reaches just inside the door and pulls out his duffle bag. He
walks quickly and quietly to the front door, hesitates only
slightly once he has the door open, then quietly exits. The
mockingbird gives one last sharp trill. After a long moment,
Sarah enters from the kitchen looking slightly pale. Ruth is
right behind her.)*

SARAH. *(Entering.)* I think maybe I better sit down in here
for . . . *(She passes her hand across her brow.)*

RUTH. *(Following her.)* Let me—

SARAH. I'm fine. I'm only . .

RUTH. *(Leading her to the sofa.)* Well, of course you're
fine. Now, you sit down right . . *(Seats her.)* . . there.
Would you like a cold washrag?

SARAH. No. I'm really . . It was just all the smells . . .
made me . .

RUTH. And I've had that stove on and it's hot in there
. . . Would you like to lie down? I'll get you a pillow if—

SARAH. No. Thank you. *(Ruth makes a quick exit into the
kitchen and re-enters immediately with a plate on which are
two pieces of toast.)*

RUTH. Here you go. *(Sarah starts to say "no.")* You nibble
on this and you'll feel a lot better. *(Puts the plate down next
to her.)* I know what I'm talking about. *(Sarah takes a piece
of toast and takes a small bite.)* You just sit right there and
eat your toast. I need to check on Mr. Tyler and see—

SARAH. Miz Biars . . could you wait a minute to do
that?

RUTH. Please call me Ruth.

SARAH. *(Smiles—awkwardly.)* It's hard to do that.

RUTH. I wish you would.

SARAH. You're . . Tyler's mother.

RUTH. Well, don't do it if it makes you uncomfortable.

SARAH. *(Takes another bite.)* I don't want Tyler to see me
not feeling too well.

37

RUTH. Of course.

SARAH. (*Still nibbling.*) The toast . . (*Nods her head approvingly.*)

RUTH. Good.

SARAH. I like your house. You've got real nice furniture.

RUTH. Thank you. Mostly odds and ends. This table, though . . I'm very fond of this table. This one. It belonged to my mother. All hand carved by her brother. (*She touches it lovingly.*) And these two chairs are from her dining room. There were eight of them and we—my two brothers and my sister, myself—each took two. I got the two with the side arms.

SARAH. They're real nice.

RUTH. (*Moving to the picture.*) This is my family.

SARAH. I saw that picture.

RUTH. (*Picks the picture up and moves to Sarah.*) It was taken not long before my mother died. She was a really beautiful woman all her life, but . . cancer. (*Looks at the picture and shakes her head, then more brightly.*) This is my sister Leah—she lives in California—and this is my brother Wendall—he lives here in Masefield, runs the post office—and this is Justin, my brother, he lives two houses down. I think Tyler looks just like him—same chin.

SARAH. Is that you in the back?

RUTH. (*Laughs.*) Yes. I had everyone standing in front of me because I was eight months—(*Hesitates only momentarily.*)—It was right before Tyler was born. (*Putting the picture back in its place.*) I must get a new frame for this.

SARAH. Miz Biars? (*Ruth turns to her.*) We're going to . . to work everything out. Tyler and me. He told me you knew. He said that last night . . that you knew and I just wanted you to know that . . that I knew you did and that . . . (*She shrugs.*) I don't know what else.

RUTH. You don't have to talk to me about—

SARAH. I know. I mean, I don't care if you don't want to, but you can—we can—if you do want to is all I'm saying. I just wouldn't want you to think I was . . trash or something like that because . . .

RUTH. No. I don't think that.

SARAH. My daddy gave me the bus money to get here. My mother and my daddy thought I ought to come see Tyler and . . and tell him so that . . (*Smiles.*) And we are going to. That's what he said . . what Tyler said.

RUTH. Well . . .

SARAH. We're going to talk some more today about it . . and we're going to go on a picnic and you can come if you want to.

RUTH. I think you and Tyler should probably—

SARAH. Oh, we can talk before we all go on the picnic. We're probably going to make our plans today. Our definite plans. You could help us do that if you wanted to.

RUTH. I'd be happy to be whatever . . use I can . .

SARAH. Tyler said you knew by looking at me that I was.

RUTH. Not . . exactly that . .

SARAH. I didn't think anyone could tell when I had my clothes on.

RUTH. I'm . . I'm sure most people can't.

SARAH. Is that the only one you've got?

RUTH. Only what?

SARAH. Is that the only picture you've got of your mother? The one over there?

RUTH. Yes.

SARAH. It's too bad it's one of her when she's dying . . . when she doesn't even look like she always did. I wish you had a better one.

RUTH. I . . suppose I simply feel . . grateful that I have one at all.

SARAH. Guess that's a lesson to us all there. We ought to have lots of pictures taken when we're healthy. For our children's sake.

RUTH. (*A smile.*) Yes. That's certainly what we should do.

SARAH. I hope you'll like me, Miz Biars. (*The two women*

*look at each other a short moment before the sound of running feet at the door draws their attention. Jean bursts into the room, flushed. Her hair is messy from running with the ribbon in it untied. She stops dead still and looks from one to the other.)*

RUTH. Jeannie? What—

JEAN. Where did he go?

RUTH. Who?

JEAN. Tyler. Where is he going?

RUTH. Nowhere. To church—Jean? Honey, what on earth is—

JEAN. I called to him, but he didn't turn around.

RUTH. When?

JEAN. Now.

RUTH. Honey, that's—

SARAH. Tyler hasn't even come out yet.

JEAN. He had his suitcase. *(She looks from one to the other and then the realization comes.)* He had his— *(She bolts from the room, exiting into the hall.)*

SARAH. Oh, my . . . oh . . .

RUTH. Now, Sarah . . don't . . *(Moving toward the hall.)* Jean only thought . . . *(Calls, moving faster.)* Tyler?

SARAH. *(Following.)* Tyler?

RUTH. *(Turns quickly to Sarah.)* You just sit back down there. I'm sure—*(Jean enters carrying a note.)*

JEAN. Mother? *(They look at her and she holds it up.)*

RUTH. What does it. . . . Let me . . .

JEAN. *(Handing her the note.)* It was on his door.

SARAH. What does it say?

JEAN. Nothing.

RUTH. *(Reading.)* "Dear Ma—I'm real sorry. I'll write more later. Ty." *(Again.)* "Dear Ma—I'm real sorry."

SARAH. He's gone? He is gone?

JEAN. Why?

SARAH. Did he leave a note for me? Is there anything for . . .

JEAN. I was just walking down the hill and I looked back over my shoulder and I saw him cutting across the corner of the school yard and I called—

SARAH. (*Moving toward the front door.*) Tyler?

RUTH. (*Stopping her physically.*) Don't, Sarah. (*To Jean.*) Did you see which way he went?

JEAN. Toward Huntington. He waved at a car and it stopped and he got in and drove off in it. Why didn't he look around when I called?

SARAH. Stop him. Can't someone stop—

JEAN. It's because of her, isn't it? He left because you came here, didn't he? You made—

RUTH. Sarah didn't—

JEAN. I don't care about Sarah. She made—

RUTH. Stop it. Sarah is a guest in our house—

JEAN. (*Begins to cry.*) But I don't want him to leave . . .

RUTH. No one does—not Sarah either—so . . blaming people is not . . (*The joyful sound of church bells is heard in the distance. Ruth moves to Jean comfortingly.*) Sh-h-h.

SARAH. He said we'd go on a picnic. (*Moves trance-like toward the screen door.*) Maybe he's . . coming back later. Maybe he is . . .

JEAN. Will he? Will he, mama?

RUTH. (*Arm around Jean.*) I don't know. I . . don't know. (*Jean buries her head in her mother's shoulder. Sarah stands looking out the door and the sound of the bells increases as the lights fade.*)

41

## ACT II

### Scene ii

*TIME: Four days later*

*SET: The same*

*AT RISE: The sound of a sewing machine is heard coming from the bedroom area. Sarah is discovered seated on the couch, dressed the same as in the last scene. She is reading a* Classic Comic *and there is a stack of comics next to her. The sound of the sewing machine is heightened 'til the lights are up to full, then it recedes to normal. Sarah finishes the comic, sighs and sadly shakes her head. Then, as though she can't really believe that that was truly the ending of the story, she turns back three or four pages and begins carefully re-reading. Ruth enters onto the front porch. She is dressed in a simple work dress, heels, and is carrying a sack of groceries. Sarah jumps up and runs to the screen door.*

SARAH. Hi.
RUTH. Hi. That's all right. I've got it. (*Ruth looks past Sarah and around the room as though looking for clues of Tyler's presence. She sees none, but really didn't expect to so the disappointment shows only a moment.*)

SARAH. You go to the grocery store on your way home?

RUTH. Sure did.

SARAH. I'll put 'em away for you.

RUTH. (*Setting the sack and her purse on the table.*) There's not much. I'll do it in a minute. (*Slips out of her shoes.*)

SARAH. (*Taking the sack and the purse.*) I can. (*Moving toward the kitchen.*) You need to sit down, I bet. You've been working hard today, I bet.

RUTH. Sarah.

SARAH. (*Turns at kitchen door.*) Yes, ma'am?

RUTH. (*Smiling.*) You can leave my purse in here if you want to.

SARAH. (*Realizing.*) Oh. (*Small embarrassed laugh.*) Oh. (*Moves back to the table with it.*)

RUTH. I did that myself one day. (*Going to the sofa.*) Put my purse in the ice box.

SARAH. Why?

RUTH. I . . I wasn't thinking I guess . . .

SARAH. Oh. Had too many things on your mind probably.

RUTH. Probably.

SARAH. Too many things to do probably. (*Standing with the sack in her arms, not looking at Ruth — quickly.*) I could go to the store for you sometimes. (*And she quickly turns and exits into the kitchen. Ruth sits, but on becoming aware of the sewing machine for the first time, she gets immediately back up and goes to the hall door.*)

RUTH. (*Calling.*) Jeannie? I'm home, honey. (*Jean calls something back.*) What? (*She listens, Jean repeats, she still doesn't understand, but decides to let it go.*) Fine. (*Moves back toward the sofa and the sewing machine continues.*)

SARAH. (*Entering from the kitchen.*) She's sewing again.

RUTH. Ah. Has . . has she been at it long?

SARAH. (*Forlorn.*) All day.

RUTH. Ah. (*"Covering."*) School clothes. She has to have a whole new wardrobe to start the fall.

SARAH. I mean, I don't know if she's been sewing all day,

but . . . (*She looks toward the hall door sadly, then after a short moment, turns back to Ruth.*) Sure hope she hasn't been 'cause that can be real bad on your eyes.

RUTH. Yes . . there's good light in there, though.

SARAH. Oh. Well, that's good. Be too bad if she had to end up wearin' glasses or going blind.

RUTH. I doubt that'll happen.

SARAH. (*Looking at Ruth's shoes.*) Those are awful pretty shoes.

RUTH. They're old. Thank you.

SARAH. I used to have a pair just like them, almost.

RUTH. You did?

SARAH. Only mine were white. —

RUTH. They did come in white.

SARAH. (*Continuing.*) — And mine had low heels. And mine didn't have — (*Picks one shoe up.*) — you know — they didn't have this open place at the toes. That's the only difference.

RUTH. (*Fighting a smile, she nods.*) Ah.

SARAH. I don't have mine no more. They got ruint when I wore 'em in the rain. Come apart. (*Jean enters into the hall doorway and leans against it with her arms folded. Neither Sarah nor Ruth notice her. She listens to them and, though she does nothing to attract attention, neither is she hiding.*)

RUTH. The rain'll do that.

SARAH. They kind of shriveled up.

RUTH. What did you do today, Sarah?

SARAH. (*Pleasantly.*) Nothin'. But I had a real nice time. I set here and waited for you to come home. Read these ol' comic books I found out on the back porch.

RUTH. I'm . . I'm sorry there's not very much for you to do here during the day.

SARAH. I like it. It's real quiet. (*Pointing at the comic she'd been reading.*) That one's got a wonderful story in it. I mean, it's just a ol' comic book, but it's about this girl who grows up in a jungle with this old man and these natives who live in the jungle with her think she's a witch—but she's not— and they try to kill her all the time, but they can't and she's beautiful. Then, she falls in love with this man who comes into the jungle and he wants to take her out but . . . but she gets burned up. By the natives. In a tree. (*Brief pause.*) I liked it. I didn't tell it right.

RUTH. *Green Mansions.*

SARAH. You read it, too?

RUTH. Well, it's based on a book and I read the book.

SARAH. And one of Jean's friends came over. (*Jean "perks up."*)

RUTH. Oh?

SARAH. But I don't know which one it was. I just heard 'em back there. She sure does have a lot of friends, doesn't she? (*Jean edges herself just a tad more inside the hallway, listening.*) She's got more friends right today than I ever even knew in my whole life, I bet.

RUTH. It only seems like a lot, Sarah . . because they move around so fast. One goes out the back door and another comes in the front and the first one comes back in a side window . . and they are always running. There really aren't so many of them.

SARAH. I don't mean I see 'em over here necessarily . . (*With a slight sense of pride at knowing someone so popular.*) . . but she's always goin' off to somebody or another's. (*Slight pause.*) 'Cept today she mostly stayed in mostly, I think.

RUTH. She's usually on the go. (*Slight pause—"casually."*) Did you write your parents today?

SARAH. (*Looking away.*) No.

RUTH. Ah. You mentioned last night you might do that is why I asked.

SARAH. (*Looking down.*) I . . didn't know what to write . . .

RUTH. Well . . I'm sure they'd like to know you're well. They might be worried.

SARAH. No . . .

RUTH. Well . . . (*She watches Sarah a moment as Sarah stands looking down at the floor.*) Sarah?
SARAH. Yes, ma'am?
RUTH. Come here.Come sit down.
SARAH. Yes ma'am. (*Moving to sofa.*) I baked a cake today.
RUTH. Good.
SARAH. (*Sitting.*) Just a ol' white cake.
RUTH. I . . I just wanted you to know that I've told people that you're the sister of a man who used to work for my husband, that you're from Georgia—which you are. . . A friend of the whole family's. It's not anyone's business, but some will ask and so I thought that might be the least embarrassing way for you. And if anyone wants to know how long you're staying . . . (*Looks questioningly at Sarah—no response.*) . . . you can just say you haven't decided yet. All right?
SARAH. All right.
RUTH. I wanted you to be prepared in case someone mentioned it. Didn't want you to be surprised.
SARAH. Yes ma'am.
RUTH. (*Pause.*) I know this is a very difficult time for you . . but you'll see . . it'll work out.
SARAH. I wish I only knew what to write them.
RUTH. (*Pats her—confidently.*) Well . . I'm sure it won't be long before we—before you hear something. . . I'm sure it won't be.
SARAH. My mother cried and cried when I told her. So did I. Having a baby shouldn't make everone so sad, should it? (*Jean quietly draws her breath in, arms wrapped tightly over her stomach. This is confirmation of her fear. She flattens herself against the doorframe.*)
RUTH. No.
SARAH. (*Looking at her hands.*) I've got the biggest ol' hands. Would you care if Tyler marries me?
RUTH. (*Gently.*) Oh, Sarah. (*Takes her hand.*) You're a very sweet and a very lovely person. So . . so don't worry about

things you don't need to. And you've got nice hands.

SARAH. (*Smiles.*) Thank you.

RUTH. You're welcome.

SARAH. He could come walking right through that door anytime, couldn't he?

RUTH. Yes. That's the way he does things.

SARAH. (*Happy in this intimacy.*) That's the way he is.

RUTH. So . . you . . you just try to relax about things. All right? (*Sarah nods, smiles.*) Now. (*This change of tone causes Jean to pull back inside the doorway where she can't be seen.*) What I'm going to do is slip out of this dress . . (*She stands.*) . . and go out and work in my garden for awhile. (*Joking with Sarah.*) Better put something back on first before I go out, though, shouldn't I?

SARAH. (*A laugh.*) Yes.

RUTH. But only for the neighbors sake. Don't want to cause any heart attacks.

SARAH. I could help you.

RUTH. No, no. I like being out there by myself.

SARAH. (*Looks down.*) Oh.

RUTH. (*Looks at her.*) I . . I don't even let Jeannie . . (*A little covering laugh.*) My "private" time. (*Jean enters and stands just inside the door. Ruth, seeing her.*) Hi, honey.

JEAN. Hi. (*Ruth begins her exit toward the hall. She makes an arc toward the screen door and glances out it almost subconsciously.*)

RUTH. Sarah says you've been working hard today.

JEAN. Yes.

RUTH. Me, too. The bank was a complete madhouse this afternoon. (*Exiting.*) Can I peek at what you're making? (*She's out.*)

JEAN. Yes.

SARAH. (*After an awkward pause.*) Sounded like you were going to burn that motor up yesterday.

JEAN. I . . want to get finished.

47

SARAH. I put a piece of cake outside your door . . but you didn't see it.

JEAN. (*She did.*) No.

SARAH. I put it over to the side so you wouldn't step in it. That's probably why you didn't see it.

JEAN. (*Looks away.*) Probably.

SARAH. (*Joking.*) 'Course it might've helped the flavor if you had of stepped in it. (*Jean glances at her and tries to smile, then looks away.*) I hope I didn't disturb you today. I tried to be real quiet.

JEAN. You don't have to be quiet.

SARAH. That's one thing I could never get the hang of. Sewing. I'm all thumbs when it comes to sewing. (*Jean looks at her, acknowledges what she has said with a facial expression, then picks up the sack of comics. Sarah "jumping to":*) I'll put those back.

JEAN. I can.

SARAH. I'm the one got 'em out. I was real careful with—

JEAN. You don't have to be—! Just stop, Sarah. Just stop it.

SARAH. (*Confused.*) What? I—

JEAN. (*Challenging.*) You didn't even tell him, did you?

SARAH. What?

JEAN. I'm not a child. I know about things . . so just stop . . . Ok?

SARAH. (*Looking down.*) 'Kay.

JEAN. (*Softer.*) My brother doesn't even know, does he?

SARAH. Yes.

JEAN. I bet he doesn't.

SARAH. I told him.

JEAN. He wouldn't have gone—(*Stops herself, looks down.*) He probably didn't believe you, that's why.

SARAH. I think he did, Jeannie.

JEAN. How do you know?

SARAH. He said he did. He said we'd work it out.

JEAN. (*Looks at her a moment, then.*) Well, then . . he will.

48

SARAH. He . . needed some time to think. That's what he said.

JEAN. He did?

SARAH. He'll be back pretty soon probably.

JEAN. I know he will. . . And when he gets back he'll . . take care of it. (*Sarah nods and smiles.*) I just want everyone to quit treating me like I'm not supposed to know anything about anything. You and mother—I'm part of this family, too—And Tyler would have told me himself if—He knew I could—(*She abruptly turns away.*)

SARAH. (*After a short pause.*) Do you care if I stay 'til he gets back?

JEAN. No.

SARAH. I wouldn't blame you if—

JEAN. You have to stay. Tyler meant for you to.

SARAH. (*Hopefully.*) Did he tell you that?

JEAN. When would he—He didn't have to tell me. (*Turns back to her.*) He left you *here*, didn't he? He wouldn't've gone off and left you by yourself someplace. He's not that kind of person, Sarah. He's my brother and I know all about him and he left you here because he knew you'd be all right here and that . . that we'd take care of you 'til . . . and when he gets back he'll expect you to be here. So you have to stay.

SARAH. I only don't want to be in your way or—

JEAN. You're not. (*Slightly defensive.*) And you didn't have to stay out here by yourself all day either.

SARAH. Oh, I—

JEAN. (*Going on.*) You could have come back in my room. Nobody said you couldn't.

SARAH. I was—

JEAN. It was Vicky who closed the door. Not me.

SARAH. Oh.

JEAN. She . . she always does that. She didn't mean to slam it either. Just the wind blew it.

SARAH. Oh. Was a nice breeze today.

JEAN. But you could've knocked if . . . (*Looks directly at*

*Sarah.*) If my door is closed, Sarah, and you need anything
. . just knock. All right?
SARAH. All right. (*Smiles.*) And the same goes for me. (*She
smiles warmly at Jean who tries to smile back, but ends up
looking down at the comics she is tightly holding.*)
JEAN. (*Indicating comics.*) I better put—
SARAH. (*Holding her hands out.*) I'll put them back. (*Jean
slowly hands them to her.*) I know right where they go. (*And
she exits, happily, through the kitchen exit. Jean stands looking after her for a long moment, then starts to exit to her
room. She stops, then goes to the phone, picks up receiver,
dials operator.*)
JEAN. Minnie? Could you ring the Holbrooks, please?
Thank you. Vicky? I can't . . I'm not coming over tonight.
—I'm just not.—We've got company, that's why.—I'm not
mad at you. That's not—Look, I don't want to talk about it.
I'm just not coming over. I'll call you. Bye. (*She hangs up,
stands a moment, then walks slowly to the screen door and
stares out as the lights fade.*)


## ACT II

### Scene iii


TIME: *Three weeks later. Late evening.*

SET: *The same.*

AT RISE: *The stage is empty with only one lamp on.
In the distance we hear the sound of carnival music.*

*After a long moment, we hear the sound of laughter over the music outside. Jean enters dressed in a light skirt and top, carrying three or four carnival "prizes". She turns the light on when she enters. Sarah follows her in, dressed similarly to the last scene with the addition of a carnival hat and she is carrying a kewpie doll. The dialogue begins before they enter.*

JEAN. He did not.

SARAH. He did so.

JEAN. (*Entering.*) Did not, did not, did not.

SARAH. (*Entering.*) Did so, did so, did so. (*Jean makes a face and a sound indicating repulsion.*) But he had real pretty eyes—shiny—and he's traveled all over the world with that circus, I bet.

JEAN. Sarah, even if he wasn't teasing, I'm not ever in one hundred million, billion years going to go on a date with him. He had dirt caked under his fingernails and . . (*Giggles.*) . . and he only had about four teeth, I bet.

SARAH. (*Giggles.*) They looked like real good teeth, though. (*They laugh at their cleverness.*)

JEAN. Now, we're not being very kind. The poor man can't help it.

SARAH. I still think he was nice.

JEAN. Wonder if mother's home yet.

SARAH. Probably still at your Uncle Justin's. It isn't very late.

JEAN. (*Calling.*) Mother?

SARAH. Well, if she's here, silly, she's asleep. Don't wake her up.

JEAN. Are you tired?

SARAH. No-o-o. (*Plopping in a chair.*) Only my dogs.

JEAN. (*Laughing.*) Your "dogs"?

SARAH. (*Holding out her feet.*) That's what they call them in the movies.

JEAN. But . . I know, but . . it doesn't sound . . I don't know. It's not a very good word, I don't think. Just not a very . . lady-like word.

SARAH. (*Lightly.*) I guess I'm not that much of a lady.

JEAN. (*After a slight awkward pause for her.*) You know, I might sneak out in the middle of the night and run off and join this ol' circus.

SARAH. The circus?

JEAN. Yes. I think it'd be fun.

SARAH. Oh, no. I'd be too scared.

JEAN. Scared? Why?

SARAH. Things might happen to you.

JEAN. That's what I want. You come with me.

SARAH. (*A smile.*) All right. If we both went, I wouldn't be too scared.

JEAN. Maybe I can be the lady who rides on the elephant.

SARAH. And you can wear one of those real pretty white sparkly costumes and those big white feathers on your head — four feet tall.

JEAN. Or I wouldn't mind being on the trapeze — floating — . . . except I don't like being up high. (*Sarah laughs.*) I'm not scared, Sarah. I just don't like it. (*Sarah continues to smile.*) It is a problem, though, isn't it? (*Jean laughs.*)

SARAH. Well, I'd be more scared of the elephant than I would of being up high.

JEAN. Elephant's are nice. You're just a scaredy-cat.

SARAH. Me?

JEAN. Want something to drink?

SARAH. (*Shakes her head "no" — looks at her stomach, touches it.*) Guess I'd have to be the clown. (*Smiles at Jean.*) Wear something baggy.

JEAN. (*Quickly changing the subject.*) I thought you won two of those dolls.

SARAH. I gave one to a little girl when we were leaving. (*Looking at the doll.*) I never played much with dolls.

JEAN. I didn't either.

SARAH. But you've got some beautiful dolls in your room — all those on the shelves . . and on your cedar chest . . .

JEAN. But I never really played with them.

SARAH. Didn't you like them?

JEAN. I kept them, didn't I? I just didn't want to play with them and get them all messy and dirty and broken. . . I liked to . . just look at them . . .

SARAH. One time we moved into an old farm house — I was about five — before daddy bought the farm he has now, and I found this great big old doll someone had thrown in the fireplace — the people who had lived there before — except it didn't have any arms or it didn't have any clothes on or anything — but I was real, real happy when I found it there . . like finding a present. I thought the little girl had left it just for me.

JEAN. Who could throw their doll away?

SARAH. I did the same thing when we moved from there. I left the doll I'd gotten for Christmas in the fireplace for the next little girl . . but I left its arms on.

JEAN. Sarah. Your mother let you do that?

SARAH. She didn't even know 'til the next day. (*Laughs.*) Boy, did I get a licking. And they never gave me any more dolls after that.

JEAN. Not ever?

SARAH. (*Shakes her head.*) I didn't care though. (*More excitedly.*) But you know what I did play with and I've still got — I should have brought them — I've got boxes of paper dolls.

JEAN. Oh, paper dolls. I used to love to play with paper dolls.

SARAH. Oh, you did? Oh, I wish I'd brought mine.

JEAN. I'd play with them for hours.

SARAH. Forever. (*They both laugh.*) I still play with them sometimes.

JEAN. Sarah, you do not.

SARAH. Yes, I do. Dress them up. . . Jeannie, what's it like to be so pretty?

JEAN. I . . Sarah, sometimes you ask — You're pretty.

SARAH. No, I'm not.

JEAN. Yes, you are. Yes, you are. Yes, you are.

SARAH. Am not. Am not. I always wondered what it'd be like. . . Did I ever show you this one? (*And she bends her thumbs back, showing Jean.*)

JEAN. That looks awful.

SARAH. You try it. (*Jean does, but is unsuccessful.*) It's 'cause I'm double-jointed there is why I can. Everybody in my family is double-jointed. My daddy can turn his head almost clean around to the back.

JEAN. He can?

SARAH. (*Nodding.*) Double-jointed in the neck. (*Jean turns her head as far around as she can.*) I saw a man break his neck once trying to do that.

JEAN. (*Turns her head quickly back.*) You did not.

SARAH. Oh, yes, I did. Right in our front yard. Standing by the front gate. Snap. It was real awful. Trying to imitate my daddy. You know what else I saw once?

JEAN. What?

SARAH. A ghost.

JEAN. (*With not great conviction.*) You didn't either.

SARAH. Well, if you're going to keep saying I didn't when I sure did, I guess I'll just have to keep it all to myself.

JEAN. There aren't any such things as ghosts, anyway. (*Slight pause — reluctantly.*) All right. Tell me.

SARAH. Not if you're not even going to believe what I say. (*She moves toward the window.*)

JEAN. Tell me. Please.

SARAH. (*Turns to her.*) Well . . . (*She goes and turns out the overhead light.*)

JEAN. Sarah, don't turn out the lights, though.

SARAH. It was one night last summer and I was sitting in

our living room at home all by myself 'cause everbody else had gone visiting into town and I didn't want to. I just thought they'd be back early like they always do, but it kept getting later and later and it was one of those pitch black, real dark nights—the moon was mostly behind the clouds. So, I was sitting there and I started getting a little bit scared 'cause I don't ever like to be in that old creaky house at night by myself. See, we don't have any neighbors for miles and miles and—oh, yeah, there'd been these murders out near there—ax murders and they'd never even caught the person who did it and—and right then I begin to hear this sound coming from out front . . wo-o-o-o-o . . like wind in the pecan trees, but not, 'cause there wasn't any wind—it was real still . . . wo-o-o-oo-o . .

JEAN. Sarah . .

SARAH. And, then, it stopped. Just like that. I could just hear myself breathing is all. Dead quiet. And, then, it starts again only louder . . and it's closer . . wo-o-o-o . . and all of a sudden, I remember. Oh, my lord, I forgot to lock the doors.

JEAN. Oh, no . .

SARAH. And I know that whoever, whatever, it is can see me 'cause I'm sitting right in the light, so I ease over . . (*And she eases over to the lamp*) . . very, very slowly, very carefully to the light and I turn it out as fast as I can. (*She turns out the light, leaving the room bathed in the light from outside, and stands for a moment.*) Then I walk as quietly as I can to the front door and the sound is getting closer and— (*Suddenly she stops and listens.*)

JEAN. (*Small little voice.*) Sarah?

SARAH. Sh-h. Do you hear that?

JEAN. What?

SARAH. (*She listens, trying to locate the direction of the sound—then quickly.*) Is the back door locked?

JEAN. (*Quietly.*) I don't—

SARAH. (*Quietly—urgently.*) Listen. Like . . like someone

dragging something heavy across the yard. (*She looks quickly toward the kitchen door, then back to the front door. Jean does the same.*) Oh, Jeannie, I can't tell—(*She looks quickly toward the kitchen door again and she holds very still, listening.*) It's at the back door.

JEAN. Sarah . .

SARAH. Oh, my lord, it's in the house . .

JEAN. (*Tiny voice.*) No . .

SARAH. It's . . it's coming in—It's coming—(*And at this point, Ruth enters through the kitchen door, making a noise as she does so. Jean immediately screams. Sarah laughs.*)

RUTH. (*Really frightened.*) What . . ?! What in heaven's . . ?! Jean Biars, what are you screaming about?

JEAN. Mother!

SARAH. (*Laughing.*) She thought—

JEAN. Sarah!

SARAH. She thought you were a ghost.

JEAN. I didn't! I—

SARAH. You what? Who's the scaredy-cat now?

RUTH. Please turn a light on, so I can see where I'm going.

SARAH. (*Quickly doing so.*) Here, I'll get it.

RUTH. (*Still not over it.*) Honestly, you two.

JEAN. (*Still disturbed by the experience.*) What were you doing in the kitchen?

RUTH. I just got back from Justin's—

JEAN. Well, why did you come through the back?

RUTH. I always come—

JEAN. Well, why didn't you call out when—

RUTH. Jean! Because it's not something I'm in the habit of doing is why I didn't.

SARAH. (*To Ruth.*) I hope we didn't scare you.

RUTH. Well, I'm not used to being greeted by the screaming meemies in my front room.

SARAH. I sure didn't mean to scare you. I thought you saw me when I was at the window.

RUTH. I did. But I still didn't expect—

JEAN. (*To Sarah.*) Oh-h-h . . you saw her coming, didn't you? You saw her coming and timed it so . . You did that on purpose. That was really mean. (*But she laughs.*)

SARAH. (*Laughs.*) Boy, your eyes were as big as saucers.

JEAN. You wait.

RUTH. Please. No getting even. My heart won't take it.

JEAN. Yes, ma'am.

RUTH. (*Touching her heart.*) It's still pounding like a hammer. (*Jean and Sarah look sheepish. Ruth attempts to cover her anger.*) How was the circus?

SARAH. Oh, it was wonderful.

RUTH. Good. (*Slight pause.*) That's a very pretty skirt, Sarah.

SARAH. Jeannie made it for me. Out of some material she had.

RUTH. (*Cool.*) Ah-h-h . . very nice.

JEAN. I . . I decided I didn't want to make that outfit out of it. It's not a very good color for me.

RUTH. (*Looks at Jean and nods for a brief moment, then to Sarah.*) Looks very nice on you.

SARAH. Thank you.

RUTH. (*To Jean.*) Did you see Vicky at the circus tonight?

JEAN. (*Slightly defensive.*) No.

RUTH. She called. Said she hadn't seen you in awhile. I told her where you went.

JEAN. (*Changing the subject.*) Mother, why don't we give Sarah a permanent wave this Saturday?

SARAH. A permanent?

JEAN. Yes, so your hair will hold curl.

RUTH. Have you asked Sarah if she wants a permanent?

JEAN. She does.

RUTH. (*To Sarah.*) Would you like one?

SARAH. I don't know.

JEAN. You do.

RUTH. I think Sarah's hair looks very nice the way it is.

SARAH. It's kind of stringy, I guess.

RUTH. No, it isn't.

SARAH. I don't really like to get permanents 'cause they smell.

JEAN. (*To Sarah.*) It'd be—

RUTH. (*Sharper than she intends.*) Jean. It's up to Sarah. Oh, dear. (*Attempt at undoing.*) Get cranky when I get tired, don't I? (*Looking around.*) Where's . . where's my book?

JEAN. I put it back in your room.

RUTH. Well, I think I better put myself back there with it. (*Turns at the door.*) Jeannie, please don't stay up much longer, sweetie. You're beginning to get circles under your eyes. Sarah, you see she goes in in a few minutes.

SARAH. I will.

RUTH. And no more scary stories.

SARAH. Yes, ma'am.

RUTH. Goodnight. Sleep well. (*She smiles at them and exits.*)

SARAH. Goodnight. (*Sarah watches Ruth go as Jean picks and straightens things up.*) She's so nice. . . . She's been so nice to me.

JEAN. (*Snaps.*) Oh, Sarah, stop being so grateful all— (*Stops herself. She looks at Sarah.*) Want to go swimming tomorrow?

SARAH. I . . I don't think I . . can.

JEAN. Why?

SARAH. I don't have a suit.

JEAN. I know that. Wear those shorts.

SARAH. They . . don't fit anymore. (*The two women look at each other for a long moment.*) You could go with your friends if—

JEAN. I don't want to go with my friends. I want to stay with you. You're my friend. (*Brief pause.*) We'll . . do something. Want to go into the bathroom first?

SARAH. No. You go on.

JEAN. I can wait. I don't mind.

SARAH. That's o.k.

JEAN. Do I have circles under my eyes?

SARAH. I can't see them. (*Jean walks toward the hall door, stops.*)

JEAN. (*Without turning.*) I like your hair. Goodnight.

SARAH. (*Teasingly.*) Jeannie. (*Jean turns.*) I'll be sure and lock the doors.

JEAN. You just wait. (*They smile at each other and Jean exits. Sarah watches her go and then goes over and picks up her kewpie doll and looks at it. Her attention is drawn toward the door by the sound of a train in the distance—two long whistles. She walks to the screen and stands looking out a moment. She remembers the screen isn't locked and quickly does so. As soon as she does this, she smiles at herself. She stands there, doll in hand, looking into the night as the lights fade. Just as the lights are almost out, the sound of the train is heard again, somewhat louder—one long whistle that increases in volume. The second whistle begins just at the blackout and lasts a long moment into the darkness.*)

### Scene iv

*TIME: Three weeks later. August. Early afternoon.*

*SET: The same.*

*AT RISE: Before the lights come up, we hear music coming from the radio. Lights up. The stage is empty. The light is white and hot. Ruth enters from the kitchen with an ironing board which she sets up and, then, exits back into the kitchen. Jean enters from the hall dressed in shorts, blouse, hair in a pony tail.*

*She is not happy to see the ironing board in the liv-*
*ing room. She goes to the radio and switches stations*
*finding something with more of a "beat." As she's*
*adjusting the sound up, Ruth enters carring an iron,*
*a sprinkle bottle and a small armload of clothes.*

RUTH. (*Seeing Jean.*) Please, don't, Jean. It's too hot. (*She*
*puts the things down and plugs the iron in.*)
JEAN. (*After Ruth has finished her business.*) Why are you
ironing then? (*Ruth gives her a look and Jean turns off the*
*radio. Jean walks to the window and looks out.*) There's
nothing to do. It's dead. Dull and dead. (*Slight pause.*)
Listen.
RUTH. (*Busy with her ironing.*) I don't hear anything.
JEAN. That's because there's nothing to hear. Everything's
dead. (*Jean wanders aimlessly around as Ruth works. After a*
*moment Sarah enters from the outside dressed in a skirt and*
*a blouse that show the beginning of her roundness. Both*
*women look at Sarah half expectantly, but she looks away*
*and they resume what they were doing.*)
SARAH. It's going to be hotter than yesterday.
JEAN. You shouldn't wear that blouse anymore, Sarah.
RUTH. (*To Jean.*) I thought you were going to wash your
hair.
JEAN. There's no reason to hurry . . I don't have anywhere
to go. I could wash it at midnight.
RUTH. No, you couldn't. And you don't go anyplace
because you won't go anyplace, so I don't want to hear it.
Sarah and I are not going to feel sorry for you. Are we, Sarah?
SARAH. (*At a slight loss.*) No.
JEAN. I'm not asking you to.
RUTH. Well, good. (*She quickly glances from one to the*
*other.*) Because we think you should go out more. (*Sarah and*
*Jean both look at her.*)
JEAN. I don't—
RUTH. (*Going on, but "keeping busy" with her ironing.*)

Sarah and I both know that girls your age need to spend time with other girls your age. Don't we, Sarah?

SARAH. (*Looking down.*) Yes'm.

RUTH. (*Takes note of Sarah's attitude, but presses on in spite of it — to Jean.*) You don't have to hang around here all the time, does she, Sarah? (*Sarah shakes her head and turns away from them.*) It isn't healthy to spend every waking minute with just one person.

JEAN. (*Fearful for Sarah's feelings.*) Mother . .

RUTH. (*Continuing with her work.*) And I think Sarah might just appreciate having some time to herself occasionally —

SARAH. (*Turns.*) Oh, I get all the —

RUTH. (*Going on — to Jean.*) — and I know your friends would enjoy seeing you again. (*She looks directly at Jean who stares at her a brief moment, then quickly walks toward the hall exit.*) I'll pin your hair in here when you're done. (*Jean exits. Ruth looks at Sarah and gives her a small smile, then returns to ironing.*)

SARAH. Did that mockingbird keep you awake last night?

RUTH. Didn't even hear one.

SARAH. Kept me awake half the night.

RUTH. They can really get going sometimes. (*Pause in which Sarah wanders as Jean did.*)

SARAH. I saw a mockingbird kill himself one time.

RUTH. (*Wanting to avoid this story.*) Would you get the hangers for me? I think I left them in the kitchen.

SARAH. (*Slowly moves toward the kitchen.*) I was out in the fields and it was late in the afternoon 'cept the sun was still up and I was walking next to the fence next to the road. And, see, the road curves and so my daddy put up a old hubcap on one of the fence poles at the curve so cars'll know to turn. . . So I was out there walking and I saw this mockingbird and he was flying directly at that shiny hubcap as hard as he could and he was pecking at it and beating his wings at it . . making a kind of screaming sound . . He just kept doing that over and over. . . And sometimes he'd even knock himself down to the ground, but he'd get up and he'd fly right back at it again . . hard . . as hard as he could . . over and over . . screaming. . . Finally he didn't get up and fly no more. . . I buried him. He was all bloody.

RUTH. (*Has gotten caught in the story in spite of herself.*) Sarah, where do you get such stories?

SARAH. It's the truth. I saw it.

RUTH. Still . . You must scare yourself sometimes when you tell things like that.

SARAH. (*A quick smile.*) Sometimes. (*The smile goes.*) I like feeling scared sometimes.

RUTH. (*Looks at her.*) Well . . you're a first rate story-teller, but . . you're just going to have to be more selective in the stories you tell Jean.

SARAH. She asks me to.

RUTH. I know, but . . oh-h-h . . for instance the other night she didn't want to come in the house by herself. . .

SARAH. Oh.

RUTH. Maybe you'll just tell her different kinds of stories from now on. I know it's difficult but you need to remember—we both need to remember—that she's a lot younger than you are. How about my hangers?

SARAH. The hangers. (*She exits into the kitchen. Ruth takes a deep breath and looks to the heavens, then resumes ironing. Sarah reenters with the hangers.*)

RUTH. Thank you. I don't know why I thought I needed to do this today of all days.

SARAH. I could do it for you.

RUTH. No. Actually ironing is the one household chore I don't really mind. I used to iron for my mother when I was a little girl. A penny a piece. It was about the only thing they could get me to do around the house. I would much rather be at my father's store, helping him.

SARAH. I worked at a store once.

RUTH. Did you?

SARAH. But I had to quit because my mother got sick.

RUTH. I hope it wasn't a serious illness.

SARAH. It was a long time ago. She's all right now. She got cured at a revival.

RUTH. Ah-h-h.

SARAH. (*Listening.*) Was that the mail?

RUTH. I didn't hear anything.

SARAH. How come you seem so much older than me?

RUTH. (*Smiles.*) You think my hearing's going with age?

SARAH. No.

RUTH. Well, I am older than you, Sarah.

SARAH. No, you just seem like you are. Ruth?

RUTH. Yes?

SARAH. I called my daddy yesterday.

RUTH. (*Looks at her.*) You did?

SARAH. Yes. But I called him collect, though.

RUTH. You didn't need to do that. . .

SARAH. I didn't want you to have to pay for it.

RUTH. I wouldn't have . . That was . . thoughtful of you. . .

SARAH. Yes. I wasn't even sure he'd talk to me, but he did.

RUTH. I . . hope it was a good talk.

SARAH. I think so.

RUTH. (*After a brief pause.*) How was he?

SARAH. He was fine. He said he was wondering where I was.

RUTH. He didn't know where you were?

SARAH. He *thought* I was here, but he wasn't exactly sure.

RUTH. Was he . . glad to hear from you?

SARAH. I think he was. He sounded like he was. My mother was. I talked to her, too. But she's got a cold.

RUTH. I'm sorry to hear that.

SARAH. She gets 'em all the time. They said . . that . . that they kind of missed me. . . I've never been gone this long before. . . Made me want to cry when they said that.

RUTH. You miss them, too, don't you?

SARAH. (*Shrugs.*) I was real happy to talk to them, but . . .

RUTH. But what?

SARAH. (*Shrugs again — slight pause.*) They asked about Tyler.

RUTH. What did you tell them?

SARAH. I said he was just fine.

RUTH. Sarah. You didn't tell — (*Jean enters with a towel wrapped around her head, comb, and bobby pins.*)

SARAH. (*Interrupting Ruth.*) And I told them all about you.

JEAN. You told who?

RUTH. (*Seeing Jean.*) Washed it already?

JEAN. Yes.

RUTH. Sarah . . Sarah called her parents yesterday.

JEAN. (*Stops.*) Why?

RUTH. "Why"? Don't be a goose.

SARAH. (*Brightly — to Jean.*) And I told them all about you, about how nice you are —

JEAN. When did you call?

SARAH. Yesterday.

JEAN. When yesterday?

SARAH. When you were watering the garden.

JEAN. You said you were going to lie down. You didn't —

RUTH. Jean. Sarah doesn't have to tell you everything she does.

JEAN. I only wanted to know. (*Looks away.*) I hope you had a good talk.

SARAH. I did. And daddy said you all sounded like you were real nice. And what else is they told me George has been coming by a whole lot, asking about me.

JEAN. George?

SARAH. That boy who used to ask me to marry him all the time.

JEAN. You said he asked you once.

SARAH. Three times.

JEAN. Well, what's he coming around for if you're going to — if you're not even there?

RUTH. Jean, would you go get a chair from the kitchen, please? (*Jean looks at Ruth and, then, starts slowly off.*)

SARAH. And they even told him I'd gone off to get married probably, but he still —

JEAN. (*Turns on her.*) I don't care.

RUTH. Jean. (*Jean exits into the kitchen.*) Sarah, I don't want you to tease her like that.

SARAH. It's the truth.

RUTH. I don't mind you telling her the truth, but please don't tease her with it.

SARAH. I . . didn't mean to. (*Jean enters with a kitchen chair which she places D.C. She sits. Sarah walks to the window and looks out. Ruth walks up behind Jean, takes the comb from her and starts combing her hair a little too roughly.*)

JEAN. Ow-w-w. (*Ruth continues to comb.*)

SARAH. (*Looking out.*) Hurts your eyes to even look outside, so bright.

JEAN. (*Pulling away.*) Mother. You're hurting.

RUTH. (*Handing the comb to Jean.*) You do it, then. (*Ruth walks to the screen door and stares out. Sarah turns and looks at the two women. Ruth drums her fingers on the door frame.*)

SARAH. (*Moving toward Jean — a gentle voice.*) My mother's got hair clean down to her knees practically. She's never cut it. Not even once. When she gets mad at my daddy, she says she's going to, but she never does. Every night on the front porch I comb it for her. (*She takes the comb from Jean and begins combing gently.*) Her hair is gray and it's real hard to get the comb through at first 'cause it's so thick. When she washes it in the summer, she sits in the yard and I comb it in the sun and in the winter, she sits in front of the stove. I always wanted her to wear it down when I was a little girl, but she wouldn't. I don't want her to anymore, though, 'cause she's too old and she'd look. . . Am I hurting you, Jeannie?

JEAN. (*Soothed.*) No.

SARAH. I wanted hair like hers.

JEAN. Just let it grow.

SARAH. (*Smiles.*) Then I can hang it out the window and some handsome prince will climb up it and rescue me.

JEAN. I wouldn't want anyone crawling up my hair.

RUTH. (*Turns, smiles.*) Besides, by the time he got up there, he'd have snatched you bald. (*Jean and Sarah laugh small laughs.*)

SARAH. Probably give you a real bad headache, too.

JEAN. And who wants someone who doesn't have the sense to go find a ladder?

SARAH. 'Cause how are you going to get back down? (*All are laughing, though not heartily, at least lightly, releasing the tension.*)

RUTH. Let him stay on the ground.

SARAH. Want me to go make some tea?

RUTH. There's a pitcher made.

SARAH. (*Holding comb out to Ruth.*) You better do this part. The last time I curled it, she wouldn't talk to me.

JEAN. That's not—

RUTH. (*Moving toward them.*) I'll do it.

SARAH. (*Hears something outside.*) Is that the mail?

RUTH. (*Taking the comb.*) May have been.

SARAH. (*Moving toward the door.*) Did he stop?

RUTH. (*Combing.*) I don't know, Sarah.

RUTH. (*Excited.*) I'll go see.

JEAN. I wish she'd stop that.

RUTH. Waiting? What do you want her to do?

JEAN. She shouldn't act like she cares so much.

RUTH. But she does. (*Pinning Jean's hair.*) Honey . . try not to be so . . short with her.

JEAN. I'm not. Sometimes she gets . . .

66

RUTH. What?

JEAN. Nothing.

RUTH. Maybe if you'd start going out a little more—

JEAN. I can't.

RUTH. Why?

JEAN. Sarah. She . . doesn't want to.

RUTH. You could, though. (*No answer.*) Why doesn't Sarah want to go out?

JEAN. You know why. People look at her. It's embarrassing.

RUTH. I see. Well, you know what I think we should do? You and I? I think we should go to the movies tonight. Just the two of us. Want to?

JEAN. What about Sarah?

RUTH. You and I need to have—(*Sarah enters from the proch, a letter in her hand which she holds up tentatively. She gives a little nervous laugh. Both women stare at her.*)

SARAH. It's got your name on it, Ruth. It's addressed to you.

RUTH. (*Walks slowly over and takes it.*) Tyler.

SARAH. (*To Jean.*) It's real thick. (*Ruth opens the letter and pulls out two folded sheets of paper. She unfolds the paper to find about five twenty-dollar bills.*)

RUTH. (*Holding the money up.*) Money. (*She looks at one of the pieces of paper and finds nothing written on it. The second sheet is the letter.*) "Dear Ma—It's late night and things are fairly quiet here. It's a real clear night. I try to imagine you looking up at the same moon, but it's difficult because I don't think this moon ever was over our house. I think someone must switch moons at the horizon. Korea is a very strange looking country. Sometimes it seems beautiful, but mostly it just seems eerie . . . lonesome. Maybe it's me who's eerie and lonesome. Just kidding. I'm in tip-top shape and am with a great bunch of guys. Ma, the money—(*Ruth glances up at them, then back down.*)—the money is for Sarah. It isn't much, but I'll send more later."

SARAH. (*Like a child.*) Oh-h-hh-h.

67

RUTH. "I know she doesn't have any and you don't have much, so. . . She should use part of it for her bus fare home."
JEAN. Home?
RUTH. "Tell her it just wouldn't work out. I think she knows that. I'm sorry, ma, for putting— (*Ruth elects not to finish this sentence.*) There are a lot of other things to say, but I don't know what they are. I miss you and I miss the cornbread and buttermilk. Maybe you could send me some. Ha ha. Write to me. I love you, Tyler. P.S. Tell my beautiful sister that I showed her picture to the guys and she can have any one of them she wants. Tell her, too, that I love her, I hope she's not too mad at me, and that I could sure use a letter from her." (*There is a silence in which they do not look at each other.*)
SARAH. Was that other piece of paper for me?
RUTH. It was blank.
SARAH. (*Smiles.*) Boy. I surely hope he's not in a place where they're fighting and killing each other. (*Jean gets the letter and walks to the window with it.*)
RUTH. Oh, Sarah. What can I . . . ?
SARAH. That's o.k. He'll probably. . . Ruth?
RUTH. What?
SARAH. Have you ever been real deep in love with someone?
RUTH. Yes.
SARAH. Have you, Jeannie? (*Jean, without turning, shakes her head.*) I was one time. When I was sixteen, but it didn't last too long. I even married him. Did you know that? Did I ever tell. . . I feel real tired.
RUTH. (*Moving to her.*) Why don't you—
SARAH. (*Holds a hand up to stop her.*) I think maybe I ought to go to my room for a minute or something.
RUTH. Let me—
SARAH. No. (*Moves to hall exit and stops.*) Do you know how old is Tyler?

68

RUTH. Twenty-five.

SARAH. Hmm.

RUTH. Whenever you feel like you want to talk . . I'm here. . .

SARAH. I want to . . for a little while, is all.

RUTH. I understand. (*Sarah exits. Brief pause.*)

JEAN. (*Her back to Ruth.*) Do you think there's fighting where he is, mother?

RUTH. We'll never find out from Tyler if there is.

JEAN. He sounds like he's lonely.

RUTH. Maybe you could write to him this afternoon.

JEAN. (*Turns to Ruth.*) I . . don't want to.

RUTH. Honey. . .

JEAN. Why didn't he write to her? He should've written to her.

RUTH. I suppose he didn't know what to say.

JEAN. He wants you to say it for him.

RUTH. Oh-h, I . . I think he knew I'd read the letter to her. . .

JEAN. But that's cruel.

RUTH. I'm not going to argue with you about it.

JEAN. He doesn't even care, mother.

RUTH. Of course, he cares.

JEAN. And you're just going to do just what he told you to, aren't you?

RUTH. What?

JEAN. Make her leave. "Here, Sarah. Here's your bus fare."

RUTH. Do you think I would—

JEAN. 'Cause if you do—

RUTH. —Jeannie—

JEAN. I mean it, mother. You make her leave and I'll—

RUTH. No one is making anyone—

JEAN. And you'd probably be glad to get rid of her, too, wouldn't you?

RUTH. Would you keep your voice—

JEAN. Then you can pretend she doesn't even exist just like

69

Tyler's doing.

RUTH. Tyler is not—

JEAN. She's going to have his baby!

RUTH. Do you want to tell the whole town?

JEAN. That's all you care about, isn't it?

RUTH. Stop this.

JEAN. Well, I hate him.

RUTH. Jean—

JEAN. I do.

RUTH. You don't. Don't ever—

JEAN. And I don't care if I never see him again. I don't care if he— (*Ruth slaps her—not hard. Jean turns away.*)

RUTH. You don't mean that and I won't have you say such a thing . . not when he's. . . I'm sorry, Jeannie, I—

JEAN. (*Her back to Ruth—quieter.*) You're always on his side, aren't you?

RUTH. No.

JEAN. You always stand up for him.

RUTH. I'm just trying to stand by him.

JEAN. (*Shaking her head.*) Oh, mother. (*Turns to her.*) She's going to have your son's baby.

RUTH. I know that. No one ever has to remind me of that fact. I know it every waking moment of my life. I can feel that baby tugging at me . . and it's my son's. But there is nothing I can do.

JEAN. Make her stay here 'til—

RUTH. I can't make her—

JEAN. She needs us.

RUTH. She has her own family.

JEAN. You just don't like her. You—

RUTH. I do. I do like her. I probably like her—her, just the way she is—beter than you do.

JEAN. Sarah's my friend.

RUTH. Tyler's your brother.

JEAN. And you don't think she's good enough for him.

RUTH. Do you?

JEAN. (*Feebly.*) Yes,

RUTH. Jean. Do you want him to marry her?

JEAN. He can't. He's in Korea.

RUTH. Would you want him to? (*No answer.*) Honey. You've tried so hard. I haven't known how to . . help you always, what to say to you . . how to explain . . I've been so worried about you sometimes . . but I have been so very proud of you, too. . . . But you can't take his place.

JEAN. I'm not trying —

RUTH. (*Going on — more firmly.*) That's all there is to it. This is between them. And it really doesn't matter what you want or what I want. It's between Sarah and Tyler and you and I have only been living in a kind of suspension between them. We have no say in what happens or what should happen here.

JEAN. Who does? Just Tyler?

RUTH. Sarah, too.

JEAN. No, she doesn't. It's all his decision. It's not fair.

RUTH. Sometimes things . . aren't. . . .

JEAN. (*Turning toward hall.*) I'm going —

RUTH. Jean. (*Jean stops.*) Tyler loves you. And he wants you to forgive him . . He asked you to in his letter. He's your brother and no matter what he's done, he'll always be your brother — your family. Other people come and go in your life, but your family is always there. Always.

JEAN. That baby is part of our family, too. (*Sarah appears in the door with her suitcase in one hand and the kewpie doll in the other. Ruth and Jean stare at her a long moment.*)

SARAH. (*Smiles — pleasant.*) I have to go back home now.

JEAN. No, Sarah. . .

SARAH. There's a bus about three-thirty.

JEAN. You can't. . .

RUTH. There's no reason to. . . . Why don't you give yourself . . this evening at least. You can —

SARAH. I think I'll go now.

JEAN. Stay. You don't have to go anywhere.

RUTH. We need—we all need—some time to talk before—
SARAH. Could I have part of that money?
RUTH. Sarah. . . The money is all yours.
SARAH. I just want enough to get home on.
RUTH. (*Handing it to her.*) You'll need it, Sarah. Tyler meant for you to have it.
JEAN. You can't just go away. Mother, tell her she can't.
SARAH. I want to, though. I want to go home . . but I've really liked meeting you. It's been real nice here and . . and thank you for letting me stay and I hope you'll come visit me sometime, too. Well. I'm not mad at anyone.
JEAN. You should be! Don't you know you should be!
SARAH. (*Smiles, shakes head slightly, puts kewpie down on chair.*) I'm just going to leave this here.
JEAN. I don't need something to remember you by!
SARAH. (*Looking at her.*) Me neither. (*Sarah and Jean hold each other's gaze a long moment.*)
RUTH. We'll . . miss you, Sarah. (*Sarah turns to Ruth and looks steadily at her. Ruth becomes slightly uneasy, looks down.*) We . . both will. . . (*Sarah starts for the door.*) Now, I'll go with you and—
SARAH. No.
RUTH. I insist. Now. I insist.
SARAH. No. (*Turns at the door.*) Bye-bye. (*She exits. Ruth and Jean stand looking after her for a long bewildered moment.*)
JEAN. (*Quietly.*) Sarah?
RUTH. Honey—
JEAN. (*Slightly louder.*) Sarah.
RUTH. Oh, my Jeannie, don't be too hurt.
JEAN. I . . can't believe . . she's just . . leaving. . .
RUTH. I tried to warn you. . .
JEAN. What? That she'd go away? Like "other people" who just come and go? Sometimes, mother, when they go . . they stay, too.
RUTH. Yes. (*Jean looks at Ruth and suddenly starts taking*

*the pins out of her hair. She moves toward the front door.)*
JEAN. Let's walk with her, anyway, mother.
RUTH. We can only go to the bus stop. You have to let her go on from there. Jean? Do you know what I'm saying?
JEAN. I want to walk with her as far as I can. *(Jean exits. The door slams. In the far distance the sound of children playing can be heard. Ruth stands only a moment, then follows Jean out the door. The sound increases and after a moment, the lights begin to fade. The light on the kewpie doll fades more slowly than the others. The sound comes up, the lights go out.)*

## END

# PROPERTY LIST

*Ii*

Pack of cigarettes
Lighter
Small suitcase
Purse with unopened letter in it.

*Iii*

(Cigarettes and Lighter)

*IIi*

Bible
Duffle Bag
Plate with two pieces of toast
Small note from Tyler

*IIii*

*Green Mansions* — classic comic
Stack of comics
Sack of groceries
Purse

*IIiii*

Two or three carnival prizes
Carnival kewpie doll

*IIiv*

Ironing board
Iron
Sprinkle bottle
Small armload of unironed clothes
Clothes hangers
Towel
Comb
Bobby pins in box
Kitchen chair
Air-mail letter from Tyler
  1 blank sheet
  5 twenty dollar bills
  1 letter

Suitcase and purse for Sarah from Ii
Kewpie doll from IIiii

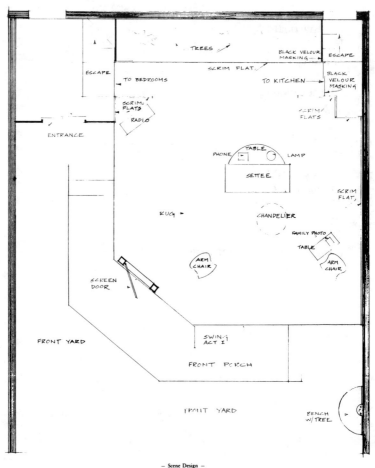

TREES

BLACK VELOUR MASKING

ESCAPE

ESCAPE

SCRIM FLAT

TO KITCHEN

BLACK VELOUR MASKING

TO BEDROOMS

SCRIM FLATS

RADIO

SCRIM FLATS

ENTRANCE

PHONE

TABLE

LAMP

SETTEE

SCRIM FLAT

RUG

CHANDELIER

FAMILY PHOTO

TABLE

ARM CHAIR

ARM CHAIR

SCREEN DOOR

FRONT YARD

SWING ACT I

FRONT PORCH

FRONT YARD

BENCH W/TREE

— Scene Design —
"A DIFFERENT MOON"
(Designed by Jim Steere
for the WPA Theatre)

76

## IF I HAD THE WINGS OF AN ANGEL

If    I    had the wings of    an    an - gel

O - ver these    pri-son walls  I would    fly

Right    in  -  to the  arms  of  my    loved one

And    there  would I   will - ing - ly   die.

# NEW PLAYS

★ **THE CIDER HOUSE RULES, PARTS 1 & 2 by Peter Parnell, adapted from the novel by John Irving.** Spanning eight decades of American life, this adaptation from the Irving novel tells the story of Dr. Wilbur Larch, founder of the St. Cloud's, Maine orphanage and hospital, and of the complex father-son relationship he develops with the young orphan Homer Wells. "...luxurious digressions, confident pacing...an enterprise of scope and vigor..." *–NY Times.* "...The fact that I can't wait to see Part 2 only begins to suggest just how good it is..." *–NY Daily News.* "...engrossing...an odyssey that has only one major shortcoming: It comes to an end." *–Seattle Times.* "...outstanding...captures the humor, the humility...of Irving's 588-page novel..." *–Seattle Post-Intelligencer.* [9M, 10W, doubling, flexible casting] PART 1 ISBN: 0-8222-1725-2 PART 2 ISBN: 0-8222-1726-0

★ **TEN UNKNOWNS by Jon Robin Baitz.** An iconoclastic American painter in his seventies has his life turned upside down by an art dealer and his ex-boyfriend. "...breadth and complexity...a sweet and delicate harmony rises from the four cast members...Mr. Baitz is without peer among his contemporaries in creating dialogue that spontaneously conveys a character's social context and moral limitations..." *–NY Times.* "...darkly funny, brilliantly desperate comedy...TEN UNKNOWNS vibrates with vital voices." *–NY Post.* [3M, 1W] ISBN: 0-8222-1826-7

★ **BOOK OF DAYS by Lanford Wilson.** A small-town actress playing St. Joan struggles to expose a murder. "...[Wilson's] best work since *Fifth of July*...An intriguing, prismatic and thoroughly engrossing depiction of contemporary small-town life with a murder mystery at its core...a splendid evening of theater..." *–Variety.* "...fascinating...a densely populated, unpredictable little world." *–St. Louis Post-Dispatch.* [6M, 5W] ISBN: 0-8222-1767-8

★ **THE SYRINGA TREE by Pamela Gien.** Winner of the 2001 Obie Award. A breathtakingly beautiful tale of growing up white in apartheid South Africa. "Instantly engaging, exotic, complex, deeply shocking...a thoroughly persuasive transport to a time and a place...stun[s] with the power of a gut punch..." *–NY Times.* "Astonishing...affecting ...[with] a dramatic and heartbreaking conclusion...A deceptive sweet simplicity haunts THE SYRINGA TREE..." *–A.P.* [1W (or flexible cast)] ISBN: 0-8222-1792-9

★ **COYOTE ON A FENCE by Bruce Graham.** An emotionally riveting look at capital punishment. "The language is as precise as it is profane, provoking both troubling thought and the occasional cheerful laugh...will change you a little before it lets go of you." *–Cincinnati CityBeat.* "...excellent theater in every way..." *–Philadelphia City Paper.* [3M, 1W] ISBN: 0-8222-1738-4

★ **THE PLAY ABOUT THE BABY by Edward Albee.** Concerns a young couple who have just had a baby and the strange turn of events that transpire when they are visited by an older man and woman. "An invaluable self-portrait of sorts from one of the few genuinely great living American dramatists...rockets into that special corner of theater heaven where words shoot off like fireworks into dazzling patterns and hues." *–NY Times.* "An exhilarating, wicked...emotional terrorism." *–NY Newsday.* [2M, 2W] ISBN: 0-8222-1814-3

★ **FORCE CONTINUUM by Kia Corthron.** Tensions among black and white police officers and the neighborhoods they serve form the backdrop of this discomfiting look at life in the inner city. "The creator of this intense...new play is a singular voice among American playwrights...exceptionally eloquent..." *–NY Times.* "...a rich subject and a wise attitude." *–NY Post.* [6M, 2W, 1 boy] ISBN: 0-8222-1817-8

**DRAMATISTS PLAY SERVICE, INC.**
440 Park Avenue South, New York, NY 10016  212-683-8960  Fax 212-213-1539
postmaster@dramatists.com  www.dramatists.com